Successful Presentations

Successful Presentations

by

Carole McKenzie

Copyright © Carole McKenzie 1993

The right of Carole McKenzie to be identified as the author of this work has been asserted by her in accordance with the Copyright, Designs and Patents Act, 1988.

First published in the UK 1993
by Century Business
An imprint of Random House UK Ltd
20 Vauxhall Bridge Road, London SW1V 2SA

Random House Australia (Pty) Ltd
20 Alfred Street, Milsons Point
Sydney, NSW 2061, Australia

Random House New Zealand Ltd
18 Poland Road, Glenfield
Auckland 10, New Zealand

Random House South Africa (Pty) Ltd
PO Box 337, Bergvlei, South Africa

Set in Bembo by SX Composing Ltd, Rayleigh, Essex
Printed and bound in Great Britain by
Mackays of Chatham PLC, Chatham, Kent

A catalogue record for this book is available from the British Library.

ISBN 0-7126-5691-X

The Sunday Times 'Business Skills' series currently comprises books on total quality management, personal skills and leadership skills.

This first class series has received a warm welcome from readers and critics alike: the opinion of Christopher Lorenz of the *Financial Times*, for example, is that it is 'excellent . . . well worth reading'. It is designed to build into an essential management library of authoritative and handsomely produced books. Each one, providing a definitive standalone summary of best business theory and practice in its field, is also carefully co-ordinated to complement *The Sunday Times* 'Business Skills' video training package of the same name produced by Taylor Made Films.

BOOKS IN THE SERIES:

QUALITY: MEASURING AND MONITORING
Tony Bendell, John Kelly, Ted Merry, Fraser Sims
ISBN 071265514X (P)

QUALITY: TOTAL CUSTOMER SERVICE
Lynda King Taylor
ISBN 0712698434

QUALITY: SUSTAINING CUSTOMER SERVICE
Lynda King Taylor
ISBN 0712655190 (P)

QUALITY: ACHIEVING EXCELLENCE
Edgar Wille
ISBN 0712698639

QUALITY: CHANGE THROUGH TEAMWORK
Rani Chaudhry-Lawton, Richard Lawton, Karen Murphy, Angela Terry
ISBN 0712698337

EFFECTIVE MEETINGS
Phil Hodgson, Jane Hodgson
ISBN 0712698736

TIME MANAGEMENT
Martin Scott
ISBN 0712698531

LEADERSHIP: THE ART OF DELEGATION
David Oates
ISBN 0712656510 (P)

LEADERSHIP: THE ART OF MOTIVATION
Nick Thornely and Dan Lees
ISBN 0712656464 (P)

Contents

Foreword

1	WHAT MAKES A GOOD PRESENTER?	1
2	THE FOUR KEY ELEMENTS OF SUCCESSFUL PRESENTATION	7
3	INITIAL PREPARATION	16
4	IMPACT	32
5	EFFECTIVE COMMUNICATION	48
6	NOTES	63
7	HOW TO CONTROL NERVES	86
8	DELIVERY	93
9	BODY LANGUAGE	112
10	VISUAL AIDS	131
11	QUESTION TIME	145
12	FINDING YOUR STYLE	163
13	OTHER TYPES OF PRESENTATIONS	170
14	QUESTIONS AND ANSWERS	200
15	ADVICE FROM THE EXPERTS	204
16	CONCLUSION	208

Index   *209*

Foreword

Having spent almost all my adult life in the field of education and training, and having trained thousands of managers in the art of successful presentation, I can still relate to this quotation by George Jessel:

> *The human brain starts the moment you are born and doesn't stop until you stand up to speak in public.*

It is a familiar feeling to everyone who has had to stand up and speak before an audience, whether it is a small or a large group. Some books on presentation skills will claim that you can totally eliminate this fear by taking certain action. I don't believe that this can ever be the case. Ask any experienced presenter if they feel nervous before a 'performance', and almost certainly they will admit they do still suffer from nerves. Most would be worried if it were otherwise.

I hope that this feeling of being nervous will never leave you. It means that you are interested enough in the subject and the occasion to be concerned about doing a professional job, and creating a good impression of yourself and the organisation that you represent.

Successful Presentations will not eliminate your fear, but it *will* show you how to avoid taking flight, and how to harness your fear into a positive force which will add energy and gravitas to your performance.

One of the most frequent questions I am asked about presentations is 'Where should I begin?' I have therefore laid out the chapters in an easy to follow order. You can select the areas which are relevant to your particular need. With this in mind I suggest that you firstly concentrate on and systematically work through chapters one to four. This will provide the 'core' of your preparation. Other factors such as incorporating visual aids and questions can be worked in later.

Where appropriate, useful checklists are included. This will provide you with a 'blueprint' on which to base all future presentations, whatever the size of your audience, the formality or informality of the occasion, or the subject.

Who should read this book?

As my presentation skills training courses have concentrated mainly on managers and directors, they are the prime audience. However, this book is equally beneficial for everyone who has to speak in public. For example, increasing numbers of men and women today have the opportunity of speaking up at shareholders' meetings, parent teacher associations, and at numerous after dinner and social events.

Successful Presentations is about helping you to improve your personal presentation performance. Giving memorable presentations will give you a great feeling of personal satisfaction. A good presenter is remembered and admired by colleagues and clients. And finally:

Good Presenters Mean Good Business

Increasing numbers of these good presenters are women. Please therefore read 'he' as 'he/she'.

I would like to thank all the men and women who have shared the pleasure of presenting with me over the years, and who have added to my enjoyment and awareness of the particular challenges facing managers in today's business environment.

1. What Makes a Good Presenter?

In a training situation, I always start off by asking the group what qualities they believe a good presenter should have. Here is a typical list of responses:

- He has something worth saying
- He has time to prepare
- He has experience
- He looks in control
- He has confidence
- He has a gift for speaking

I then ask the group what makes speaking difficult for them.

The responses generally are the opposite of the above. For example, I have little time to prepare, and I end up with inadequate information, poor notes and visuals; or, I know my material, but nerves take over and I feel my performance doesn't do me credit.

Probably the most frequent complaint is lack of time to prepare. What you learn from this book will help you cut preparation time to a minimum. Often the difference between a good presenter and a poor one is this element of preparation.

Before we begin I'd like briefly to outline the qualities which I regard as being important in a good presenter: when you stand up to speak in public you are disclosing your personality. There are certain personal qualities which if cultivated can improve performance and allow your unique personality to reveal itself to the audience.

Qualities

Professionalism
It should be clear to your audience that here is a presenter who has taken the time and trouble to prepare well.

- He knows the subject and how it relates to his audience.
- His materials, for example visuals and handouts, are relevant and well designed.
- He has clear objectives, and uses signposting to lead the audience to a satisfactory conclusion.
- He presents the information in a clear, logical and interesting manner.

All of the above will be lost if the presenter does not also display sincerity.

Sincerity

- He is honest with the audience.

If you set yourself up to be something you are not, for example 'an expert' in a particular topic, your audience will quickly catch on and spot the fake. Unfortunately a frequent result of this is that the audience now sets itself up to expose you, or trip you up. Sincerity is a quality which the audience can 'sense' in a speaker. It's the enthusiasm and passion that accompanies his words and actions, and his genuineness in showing interest in the audience and their feelings and concerns. He has regard for his audience and a belief in the value of his message: it is not some half-baked idea dreamed up in five minutes, but a well thought out strategy composed with the feelings and needs of the audience in mind.

Professionalism and sincerity will help the speaker forge a link with his audience. The audience will respect these attributes, and be willing to hear him out.

Finally, the element which together with the above can

transform a mediocre performance into a memorable one: conversation.

Conversation
Many presentations fall down on this element because of the attitude of the presenter, for example if the presenter views the audience as a 'whole' and not as a collection of individuals. When you are speaking to a group, each person in the group should feel that you are addressing them personally. Obviously the smaller the group the easier this will be, but it is also possible to achieve it with a larger audience.

To give you an example, last year I saw a marvellous demonstration of how this particular element can work to the speaker's advantage. I had the pleasure of attending a large gathering to hear Rosabeth Moss Kanter, a Professor at the Harvard Business School, and a couple of her colleagues talk about managers and change. The first two speakers were interesting and put across their information well. One spoke from behind a table, the other from a lectern. Then Rosabeth Moss Kanter stood up and walked across the stage to the microphone. Taking it in her hand, she came right out to the front of the platform and had a 'conversation' with the audience. Sitting near the back of the hall, I could detect a change in the audience when she began to speak. The audience had listened politely to the previous two speakers, with little reaction. Now they seemed less fidgety, they were sitting up in their seats, hanging on to every word, nodding and responding to her comments.

This demonstrated to me the powerful effect this key element plays in public speaking. I saw it at first hand. The first two performances were good, but more like lectures, with little audience rapport or interaction. The last performance was memorable.

To sum up
A professional approach towards your material and your audience will gain you their respect and admiration.

Being true to yourself, emphasising your positive attributes, and showing how your knowledge and strengths can help the audience, will help build credibility and sincerity.

Treating the audience not as a group but as individuals will forge a bond and form a rapport, which will help you to fulfil your presentation objectives.

I was particularly interested in the Rosabeth Moss Kanter demonstration as I had written to her some months before, asking for advice for new presenters, for my book *Presenting for Women in Business*. I think it sums this section up beautifully.

Here is what she advised:

> *This first and most fundamental skill is to be an expert and to **know your subject well**.*
>
> *The second important skill is self-confidence – which shows in the ability to **claim all the space** on a stage or at the head of a conference table; to move around the room; to recover quickly from mistakes and even make a joke out of them; and to be flexible enough to bring in new material spontaneously or to make changes on the spot.*
>
> *The third key skill is to **empathise** with the audience. It is important that their needs be met and that the emotional state of the audience be kept first and foremost in the presenter's mind. It is up to the presenter to relax a tense audience with a joke, to reassure people that the difficult subjects will be handled well, and to **treat members of the audience as individuals** who are potential friends and supporters.*

Why Not Send a Memo?

There are many occasions when a memo, letter or telephone call will serve the communication need. Only you will be able to make this decision, but here is a simple checklist to help you determine if a presentation is warranted.

Information Needs

- Are there important information needs? For example, are organisational or professional policies/procedures being put into

effect. e.g. new company expenses policy, early retirement packages?
- Are new production data needed by other people or departments in order to ensure adequate job performance. e.g. stock control?
- New research information becomes available to inform staff of new procedures and operations. e.g. safety, crime statistics?
- Do managers need to inform staff of new procedures and operations. e.g. reduction in overtime?
- Is there a need to make technical information more meaningful to non-technical staff. e.g. helping enquiry staff identify customer requirement?

Belief-Changing

- Are there important attitudes and beliefs which need to be changed?

For example, in today's business climate many managers are being given the task of informing key personnel of planned staff reductions. Whether or not this can successfully be communicated will partly depend on the manager's belief in the worth of the action, and also whether they accept that the action is correct.

Belief-Strengthening

- Are there important beliefs and attitudes that need to be re-emphasised and strengthened?

Changing beliefs means communication against initial neutrality or opposition. **Strengthening** outlooks means deepening already held perceptions. For example, assuming that staff have accepted a new policy on reduced overtime, is there a need for management to make employees believe it even more keenly, in order to get better performance within the reduced operational time available?

Action Needs

Are there important actions necessary to enable implementation of these new policies, guidelines and procedures? For example, information gathering, objective setting, training, monitoring.

Each time you are asked to give a presentation, ask yourself 'What outcome do I require?' You will find that the answer will fall into one of the above categories.

The purpose of giving the presentation is to effect change in your audience – ask:

What do I want this audience **Feeling**, **Believing**, **Seeing** and **Doing** differently as they go away?

Value checklist

A presentation is particularly valuable when:

- an atmosphere of openness is desired – this enables a free and frank exchange of ideas.
- the subject matter is of a sensitive nature. (If confidential, a one-to-one situation may be best.)
- it is essential that everyone gets the information at the same time, e.g. redundancy notice
- warmth is called for – personal qualities are important here. Opportunity for feedback.
- feelings need to be strengthened, which is difficult to achieve with written communications.
- decisions need to be communicated quickly – important if deadlines are essential.
- the situation dictates maximum understanding – allows for questions, clarification of facts.
- the communication calls for personal attention, authenticity and clout. e.g. messages from chairman.
- outlining targets, cohesion of groups – common goals – teamwork.

At this stage, you will have decided that a presentation is necessary, and you will have some idea of the reasons for giving it.

This is a good starting point to consider the four key elements to successful presentation.

2. The Four Key Elements of Successful Presentation

The four key elements to successful presentation are:

The Target
This is simply your objectives. Ask yourself the following questions:
    Why am I giving this presentation and what do I want to achieve at the end of the day?

The Receiver
- Who is the audience?
- Why are they attending the presentation?
- What do they want to hear?

Impact
What steps will I have to take in order to impress the audience?
    How can I establish my authority, credibility, sincerity in order to gain their attention and respect?

Methods
What methods will I adopt in order to:

- Gain and hold their attention and interest?
- Put my views across simply and effectively?

- Organise my material and visual aids to best effect?
- Routemap my script so that it has structure and follows a logical sequence?
- Receive feedback?
- Make it memorable, and, if not giving bad news – enjoyable.

Firstly I would like to look at the target and the receiver. Impact and method will be covered in later chapters.

The reason for starting with these two elements is that these are very often the areas which are hastily covered or completely overlooked in the initial planning stage. Up to this point you have let your mind roam over the subject and some of the reasons why you might give this presentation. Now is the time to get down to business, to start planning in more detail.

'If you don't know where you are going you will end up somewhere else.' This is sound advice. How often have you sat in an audience where the presenter has launched into his presentation with obviously no thought to where he is eventually destined? Even worse, been in an audience where the presenter has appeared to know his destination, but has allowed his audience to guide and often lead him off in a completely different direction. This is a waste of time for both the presenter and the audience. The first step in planning therefore should be to identify the target (the objective(s)).

Check that your objectives are 'smart', i.e. **specific**, **measurable**, **agreed**, **realistic** and **timely**.

Specific

Sit down and try to put your objectives into a clear statement. Some people like to write this on a card and keep it in front of them as they progress through the preparation stages. A common mistake here is to write too much detail. Keep it clear and simple.

Examples

- To persuade management to adopt a new quality programme
- To inform staff of changes in company benefits

- To motivate the sales team to increase sales

This statement should be the end result of your presentation, i.e. what you want to achieve.

Measurable
How will you know you have been successful? When we have a target in mind we usually also have some idea of desired outcome. For example the objective of persuading management to adopt a new quality training programme could be immediately measurable, for instance by asking for and gauging their support by a show of hands. If they need time to think about it, then feedback could come in the form of a further meeting or by questionnaire. For those occasions, such as motivating to increase sales, where the results are not instant, then measures must be built in, e.g. agreement to meet again and review the sales figures in three months' time. Objectives that cannot be measured are worthless.

Agreed
There are several points to be considered here:

The first is that if you are asked to give a presentation

a) by your divisional director, or another person within your organisation:

- Check out the objectives with him
- Clarify any areas which are not clear: ensure that you both have the same understanding of the target

b) at a conference to speak to the audience on your area of expertise:

- Check the objectives with the organisers
- See any literature on the event – this often will contain the information you need
- If necessary speak to other presenters, to avoid confusing

objectives and overlapping of material. (Absolutely essential if you are involved in group presentations or panels)

c) You are asked to speak at a social event, an after-dinner speech for the round table, or a parent-teacher social. Your objective here may simply be to entertain!

Realistic
This means taking into account the time you have available to speak, and tailoring your talk so that it can be achieved successfully in the time allotted. This is why it is so important to make your objectives simple – don't be too ambitious. For example, if you are asked to speak about the latest range of computer software packages – as an expert, it is tempting to want to tell them every detail about every product. This may be possible if you have unlimited time available.

Ask yourself if you can realistically give a good account of ten products in the space of 45 minutes?

Far better to give some general background information on the range available, and then concentrate on a few of the key products. Supplementary information can always be given in the form of handouts or product brochures.

Timely
Time is one of the scarcest commodities in business life. It is rare to be given *carte blanche* when asked to speak to a group, and when a specific time has been set, your audience will expect you to keep to it. Keep this in mind when considering your objectives.

You have now given some thought as to why you are giving the presentation and what you are trying to achieve.

The next step is to look at the audience. Who are these people, and what do they expect to get out of the presentation?

The Audience
The receivers of your communication are the audience. The more you know about the audience and their reasons for attending, the more successful you will be in tailoring the presentation to their

The Four Key Elements of Successful Presentation

needs. The audience may consist of people that you have already met, colleagues, established clients and customers. Often, we know little or nothing about the audience and it is impossible to gain this information before the event. Some years ago, a colleague of mine learned this lesson the hard way. He was asked along to his son's school to talk about the benefits in implementing the latest computer software. Being a computer specialist he brought along the latest desktop publishing packages for demonstration. The school intended to transform all its printed material, including the school magazine, to a more professional level. He spoke enthusiastically and gave an excellent demonstration but by the end of forty minutes, most of the audience were confused, mainly by his language. The reason was that he had not considered them. He assumed that they had at least some technical knowledge, and that they were familiar with the jargon he used. This is a common fault with 'specialists' particularly when speaking to non-technical audiences. In this instance he was able to redress the balance. His excellent demonstrations spoke for themselves. Unfortunately he used up a lot of valuable demonstration time in having to go over previous information. The school did successfully adopt the new system but on another occasion, for example with a non-technical potential customer, he might not have achieved the same result.

In this situation, he could have established at the start of his talk the level of experience of the audience and then have adjusted his language and pace accordingly.

When you cannot get information about the group before the event you could adopt this strategy, i.e. ask the question – 'How many people are familiar with . . . ?' This method is also suitable for the formal business audience.

If it is a small group, you could ask each member of the group to give you that information which will help you as the presenter. 'It would be helpful to myself and the rest of the group if each of you could tell us a little information about yourself . . .'

Ask for information which will tell you what you need to know, e.g. technical, non-technical, size of company, their position, objectives for attending. This is useful in the small group situation, and I find it particularly useful in training sessions. Armed with this information I can select an appropriate starting point for the group learning process. It is also useful to know about prior knowledge or experience of the subject. The presenter can smooth the communication path by understanding and being aware of why people may feel or act in a certain way; some may feel threatened if they have had bad experiences in a similar situation. An example might be the manager who attended a similar meeting at his last company, and was told that his services were no longer required, or the potential customer at an informative produce demonstration who was presented with the hard sell.

Often when there is a large audience the event is organised so that delegates can register and meet for coffee before the presentation. This is an excellent time for you, the presenter, to arm yourself with some information. You can mix with the audience and ask a few informal but useful questions, such as why they are attending, what they hope to get out of it, names of their companies. It is also useful if you can memorise a few names and faces. At the very least you may be able to incorporate some of this information into your talk: 'I was speaking to someone earlier from IBM, they already use this method with great success . . .' It helps to build rapport, can add gravitas, and gives the audience the feeling that you have done your homework.

If you have a projected date for your presentation, one way of gaining information about your audience is to ask them to fill in a questionnaire and send it back to you before the event. This information will help you plan an audience profile and tailor your material. This is a particularly good method if you need to compile statistics to present to the group; set up syndicate groups for discussion after the presentation; or compile a list of questions to be answered. On most occasions, you will have time to find out about your audience.

Audience Profile

1. Who do they represent (company, organisation?)

2. What are their job titles, responsibilities, background, levels of knowledge, education, ages?
3. Is it a mixed audience or all male/female?
4. Is it a racially mixed audience?
5. How technical will the presentation be?
6. Is there a political factor?
7. What approach should I take, informal/formal?
8. What are their objectives?
9. What is the likely mood, receptive or hostile?
10. What's in it for them. i.e. What's the Hook?
11. How important is the presentation to decision making?
12. What do I expect from them in the way of response or action?
13. How many people will attend?
14. Any other considerations?

Use this checklist as part of your presentation preparation. The more you can find out about your audience the more you can tailor the material to their needs. One way of doing this is to send a questionnaire to clients before the event (you can delete sections, according to the purpose)

Audience Profile – Customised

This questionnaire is designed to help us tailor our presentation material to the needs of your group. Please answer the questions fully, and return to our office.
Thank you for your help.

- Please send any available printed material on your company, staff, products, equipment, training.

1. What are the objective(s) of the meeting?
   _____
   _____

2. What are the characteristics of your average member?

Sex_____   Job title_____

Main responsibilities
_____

3. How many people will be in the audience?
4. What do the audience expect to get out of the meeting?
_____
_____
_____

5. What are the top three challenges or problems faced by members of the group?
_____
_____
_____

6. What is the overall opinion regarding the subject, e.g. favourable, hostile.
_____
_____

7. What facts should I know about your group before addressing them?
_____
_____
_____

8. Are there any particular issues/topics that you think I should cover during my talk?
_____
_____
_____

9. Am I the only speaker, or are there others?
(If so, please send the programme agenda)
_____

10. Will there be any special guests?
Please explain:
_____
_____

You can make up your own questionnaire to get the specific information you require to prepare thoroughly. For example question 10 – special guests may include the decision maker, the Managing Director or Chairman. You need to know this information!

3. Initial Preparation

Information Gathering

It is now time to start gathering your information on the topic and to start the initial preparation work. This stage involves sitting down and thinking about every aspect of the event. You have already clarified the two most important areas, i.e. audience and objectives. The next question is, what information are you going to include in your presentation?

Where to find information:

- Your own or other companies' literature
  e.g. annual report and accounts, product brochures
- Company/public libraries
- From your own experience of similar events, or from speaking to other people in your company who have a particular knowledge of the subject or of the particular audience

The latter information will prove most useful. For example if colleagues already have experience of a similar type of audience, then they may be able to advise on any particular biases, or even on the types of questions or objections which may be raised.

Consult everyone you think can be of assistance in compiling your information, read up on the topic, and then start putting your ideas in writing.

A quick and simple way to get your mind working on the subject is to brainstorm your ideas. Take some time to think about the subject in a general way, let your mind roam around the general themes. Then take a piece of paper, write down the topic heading and let your ideas flow. Don't write sentences, just key words, and don't try to categorise them at this point, write them down as they emerge. After a few minutes you'll find that you have covered the page. Stop and look at your efforts. You will probably see that you can now subdivide the ideas into categories. Some will naturally fall into place, but others may be totally irrelevant – delete these.

For the purpose of illustrating this concept, I am going to use the theme graphology (the study of handwriting). To assist continuity I will use this subject as an example throughout the book. I have chosen graphology because of my particular interest in it and also the fact that it can be viewed on both a formal and informal business basis.

Example
Brief: To give an information talk to personnel managers and recruitment staff.

Subject: Graphology

Objectives: To inform managers of the benefits of using graphology as a recruitment tool.

Time: 40 Minutes: (30 minutes presentation, 10 minutes questions)

The following shows some of the ideas which I might jot down to start my preparation.

Initial Brainstorming Ideas – Subject: Graphology
Handwriting   Brainwriting   Training   Saudek   Michon

Personality   Health   Jung   Illness   Compatibility

Sex   Pulver   Statistics   Europe   USA

German/French Schools   Rhythm   Size   Crepieux-Jamin   Klages

Zones   Business Application   Capital Letters   Signatures

Stroke   General Impression   Spacing   Speed   Slant

Examples   Recruitment   Crime   Pressure   Health

From my ideas you can see that there is a lot of information here. Probably enough to keep a presenter talking for several months. We therefore need to edit this information down to our time limit of 30 minutes. This we will do later. Meanwhile we have plenty to be working on.

The next step is to have some sort of structure or skeleton to work from. Peter Morgan, Director General of the Institute of Directors, advises that a presenter should:

Tell them what you will tell them
Tell them
Tell them what you've told them

This is good advice, and is a method used by newsreaders. When you turn on the evening news, the presenter gives some punchy headlines to arrest our attention. Then he goes on to build this up with more facts, and finally he gives a brief roundup on what has been covered. This is a simple format which you should use for every presentation, no matter what the subject. Incidentally it is also one which works well for written communications such as reports.

Structure

	% of presentation time
Tell them what you'll tell them (The 'headlines')	15%
Tell them (The body)	75%
Tell them what you've told them (The summary)	10%

The recommended proportion of the total presentation time spent in each section is shown above.

Much research has gone into the ideal length of a presentation. Some specialists believe that 17 minutes is the optimum to retain audience attention and interest. Most managers have experienced boredom and have shut off during a short speech, and yet have remained alert and interested in another lasting several times as long.

Therefore, with regard to length: if you make it interesting, they will listen to you.

- Take into account your objectives
- Work to the minimum time required to get your message across
- Allow time for incorporating visuals
- Always add a period for questions.

Most business presentations last between 30 and 45 minutes, followed by 10–15 minutes questions. There are so many other factors which affect timing that there are no hard and fast rules, except that you always follow the advice above, and that when you decide on the timing – you adhere to it!

Therefore my graphology example would mean roughly:

Introduction	5 minutes
Body	22 minutes
Summary	3 minutes

At this initial preparation stage it is useful to refer to your list of ideas and jot down any key areas which you feel could be used for example as an opener, or perhaps some information which would fit nicely into the summary section.

To sum up so far:
We have now:

- Identified the presentation objectives
- Conducted an audience profile. Taking the graphology example, it would be useful to know what experience, if any, the managers have of this subject, also any biases.

- Roughly allocated ideas to the areas of structure, – intro – body – summary.

Divide up the available time to these sections.

Let's now look at the structure in more detail. The following is the minimum information required in each of these sections.

The Introduction

- If appropriate, inform the audience about yourself
- Say how long you will take
- Give ground rules for questions
- Introduce the subject and your objectives
- Hook their attention

The Body

- State your key points – as you build them up, make sure everything you say has a purpose
- Offer evidence
- Make it interesting

The Reprise and Close

- Recap the key points
- Make sure you put them in the context of your presentation
- Close with a strong sentence or statement
- Make your call for action
- End on a high, a positive note; never just come to an abrupt end!

The first and last sentences of a presentation are crucial. The importance of a clear and resounding first sentence and a well rounded finale cannot be over-emphasised. You must capture their attention at the beginning, keep them interested throughout the body, and leave them satisfied at the end.

The Opener

The purpose of the opening of the presentation is to hook the attention of the audience, to make them sit up and listen to what you have to say.

When you step out front to begin there are several things that you can do to set the tone:

- Stand tall with good posture; head up and look at the audience. Pause before you begin. (This will alert them to the fact that you are about to start.)
- Never begin to speak if the audience are restless. For example, once when sitting in an audience I missed hearing the name of the speaker simply because he had started his talk when some members were still sorting out their seating arrangements or ploughing through newspapers and company brochures.

The Hook

A hook is a statement or an object used specifically to get attention. Hooks are used, for instance, on television, radio, newspapers, magazines and billboards. Their purpose is to arrest our attention and stir up interest to find out more information. Newspapers always use hooks – in the form of headlines. A good presentation should also contain a hook.

To help you find your hook, ask yourself the following questions:

- What is the most unusual part of your subject?
- What is the most interesting and exciting part?
- What is the most dramatic part?
- What is the most humorous part?

If any of the above are relevant to your subject, reduce each answer to a sentence. Next, look at the sentences that you have come up with, and check them against the following questions.

- Does the hook lead to your objective?
- Does the hook relate to your approach?

- Does the hook relate to your audience?
- Can the hook form the first words of your message?

Use this three-point technique to test the most suitable hook:

1. You make an interesting impactive remark
2. You link, skilfully, this first sentence to your subject
3. You involve the audience in both the opening remarks and your subject.

There are many different types of openings, which are discussed in detail in Chapter 4. Here are a few examples:

Quotation
I am particularly fond of this method, but only use a quotation if it is relevant to your subject and always try to attribute the quotation to its true author. If in doubt, you could try: 'Was it George Bernard Shaw who said . . .' or, 'I believe it was Winston Churchill who once remarked that . . .' If you are attributing the quote to someone in your own lifetime, 'I once heard Sir John Harvey-Jones remark that . . .' This goes down well, and nobody can disprove it!

Story
Tell a short story that relates to your theme. Use short simple sentences and get to the point quickly. A personal experience told as a story can create intimacy with your listeners. Sometimes on a training course I tell the group about my first experience of nerves while doing teacher training. During this training I gauged my progress by noting which, and how many of my body parts shook, when standing in front of the class or writing on the board. It read: First year: whole body shake, including voice. Second year: One side of body arm and leg. Third year: great progress, usually only one leg. Fourth year: No visible outward signs, but headache caused by thumping heartbeat picked up by eardrums.
  Revealing something personal creates closeness with the

audience. Audiences love self-disclosure as long as it is relevant to the subject.

Taking my graphology example, the following might be a suitable story for my presentation. It can be particularly relevant to this subject as people are generally wary of adopting new ideas.

The sceptics are all those who have stood aloof, which is reminiscent of the story told of Charles Lamb, who was said to have declared his aversion for a stranger. 'But you don't know him' pleaded his interlocutor, 'let me introduce you.' 'No, no' objected the essayist. 'If I should know him, I'm apt to like him.'

Direct Question

This is also a useful start to the presentation. As mentioned earlier, if you have not had an opportunity to gain information about your audience before the event, then a few well placed questions at the beginning could help. For example, 'Is everybody here from marketing?' – 'How many of you are in sales?' 'Are you all familiar with this equipment/method/procedure?' or for my example:

'How many people have heard of graphology?'

Rhetorical Question

Do you know what most women fear most? According to studies, speaking in public is top of their dread list, followed by death, then rats.

The rhetorical question means that you pose the question – then answer it.

Statement of Need or Problem

'The situation is this . . .'

Show how the subject can affect the audience

'Computer software theft is currently . . . we need to reduce this figure by . . . failure to do so will adversely affect . . .

Direct Statement of Thesis
'It is my belief that more women would return to work if better childcare facilities were available.'

Statement to be Opposed
'Ben Jones has stated that production figures are down by 20 per cent from last year . . . I am here today to prove to you that the figure is nearer 40 per cent.'

Explanation of a Title
'*Quotable Women* . . . is an interesting book which contains quotations exclusively by women.'

Use an Exhibit/Model/Visual
'The brochure you see here . . .'

Once you have decided on your hook you can then proceed to the remainder of the introduction.

Hook
Start with your hook. Speak to the back of the room – be clear and positive.

Introduction
Tell them your name, and if relevant, your job title, company and a little background information about yourself. (This helps establish credibility.) Usually the presenter has been asked to give the presentation because he is the person who has more experience in the subject to be presented. This should be brief, and should reassure the audience. The audience should be thinking to themselves: here is someone who knows what he is talking about.

Subject
Give them the title of your presentation and make it provocative. The title acts as a stimulus; it should play to your purpose and, ideally your point. Give your audience clear signposts. Tell them where you intend to take them within your subject. Signposting

establishes several important factors. It shows that you know where you are going, and that there is a logical progression within your talk; and it also defines the limits in which you will work. Tell them how long the presentation will last.

Humour
Don't use humour just for the sake of it. If it is appropriate to your subject and audience, then use if carefully. There are several points to watch here:

- Make sure your jokes are in good taste, i.e. nothing sexist, racist, ageist. If there is any doubt that you might give offence, even to one person in the audience, leave it out.
- The safest joke is about yourself.
- An original joke works best, because your audience will not have heard it before. Avoid puns and clichés.

To give you an example of this: some years ago I was asked to speak at a seminar aimed at people who had or were about to set up their own businesses. I was there to speak about client presentations. The speaker before me covered all the financial aspects of tax and VAT. As this session had got quite heavy, with lots of doom and gloom about the dreaded VAT man's visit, I decided to begin my presentation by telling them a humorous story that happened to me when my company, Communication Works, was first formed.

'I can empathise with your feelings about the initial VAT man's inspection, but they really can be quite sympathetic . . . I can remember . . .'

I then went on to tell them my experience. I had arranged with my accountant for her to come to the office with all the documentation half an hour before the inspector was due. She duly arrived and we double checked all the paperwork. This done, we decided to calm our nerves with a glass of Sancerre. We had just finished this, when the inspector arrived. We got the paperwork out, answered all the questions and things seemed to be going well. I offered him a glass of wine and he accepted – we would also have one, so I decided to open another bottle. We had the wine, and in no time the inspection was complete and by all accounts successful! When the inspector left, elation took over and we decided to finish the bottle of wine. I poured it out and we toasted the VAT man . . . only to discover that when I had opened the second bottle of wine, far from being Sancerre it had been apple juice. Unfortunately when I had poured our second glass it was the real McCoy – the inspector was the only person to sample the other. Despite that, he didn't complain!

I could then link this anecdote in to what I had to say:

'As in the case of the VAT inspector, often we mean well, but could do better if we spent more time in preparation . . . preparation is an important element in client presentation.'

Using this approach did several things:

- By using a real life situation which was of interest to the audience, it put them onto the same wavelength. A VAT inspection was something we would all experience. This built a bond and a rapport with the group, enabling them to see me as someone who understood their concerns.
- Humour is often a good ice-breaker, when used in this sort of context. They laughed at the situation, which can be particularly welcome to the audience when the speaker before has presented heavy statistical material.

Note: I had not planned this opener, but rather one emphasising preparation, but on this occasion the anecdote was relevant. I changed my opening as I sat on the stage, listening to the speaker before me, when one of the members of the audience raised the question of the VAT inspection.

So part of your preparation is to be a little flexible. Don't be so rigid that you can't deviate at all from your original script.

- If possible, if you are one of several speakers, find out what the others are talking about – even a brief outline is helpful. This will help effect a smooth change-over to the next topic. Humour is a valuable addition to most presentations, as long as they observe the above rules.

Examples
Using examples is an excellent way of keeping attention and interest, if you follow these two guidelines:

- The example should be a typical, not exceptional one.
- Use enough examples to constitute a fair sample. You may need to use additional statistical information to support the conclusions you draw from one example.

Statistics

- Make them meaningful. Give examples.
- Use only a few statistics at a time. Break the monotony by using an anecdote or a visual aid.
- Use visuals to present statistics. Write large bold figures on the flipchart. To dramatise figures, use pictures and symbols instead of words.

The following three checklists will help you with your presentation.

1. Preparation Checklist
2. Venue Checklist
3. 'What If' checklist

Preparation Checklist
Title of the presentation
Objective(s)?
Audience – complete audience profile
Time?
Audience objectives (What's in it for them?)
How will I open?
What are the key points?

Do I have a logical structure?
How will I close?
How will I build rapport?
How will I add interest?
What visuals will I use?
What equipment?
How will I handle notes?
Handouts?
What are their possible questions/objections?
What approach will I take?
How will I sell the benefits?

Venue Checklist
It is important at this stage that you see the venue, if this is possible. Look around the room and check the following:
Most suitable room layout for the occasion?

Lighting: Is it adequate? – Controllable – by whom? This is important if you intend using 35mm slides. Can the room be darkened easily?

Ventilation/Air Conditioning: Is this easily accessible and controllable? Particularly relevant if it is a large group.

Electrical: Are there sufficient power points for your purpose? Are your cables long enough? Available extension leads?

Equipment: Inspect the equipment to be used and ensure that it is in working order. Overhead projector, spare bulbs. Flip chart. Check it has all its parts. Projection screen. If it is a retractable one – examine it.

The initial preparation stage is also the time to think about seating arrangements.

The following are some of the most common seating arrangements used, with the U-shaped format being most suitable for small group presentations.

INITIAL PREPARATION

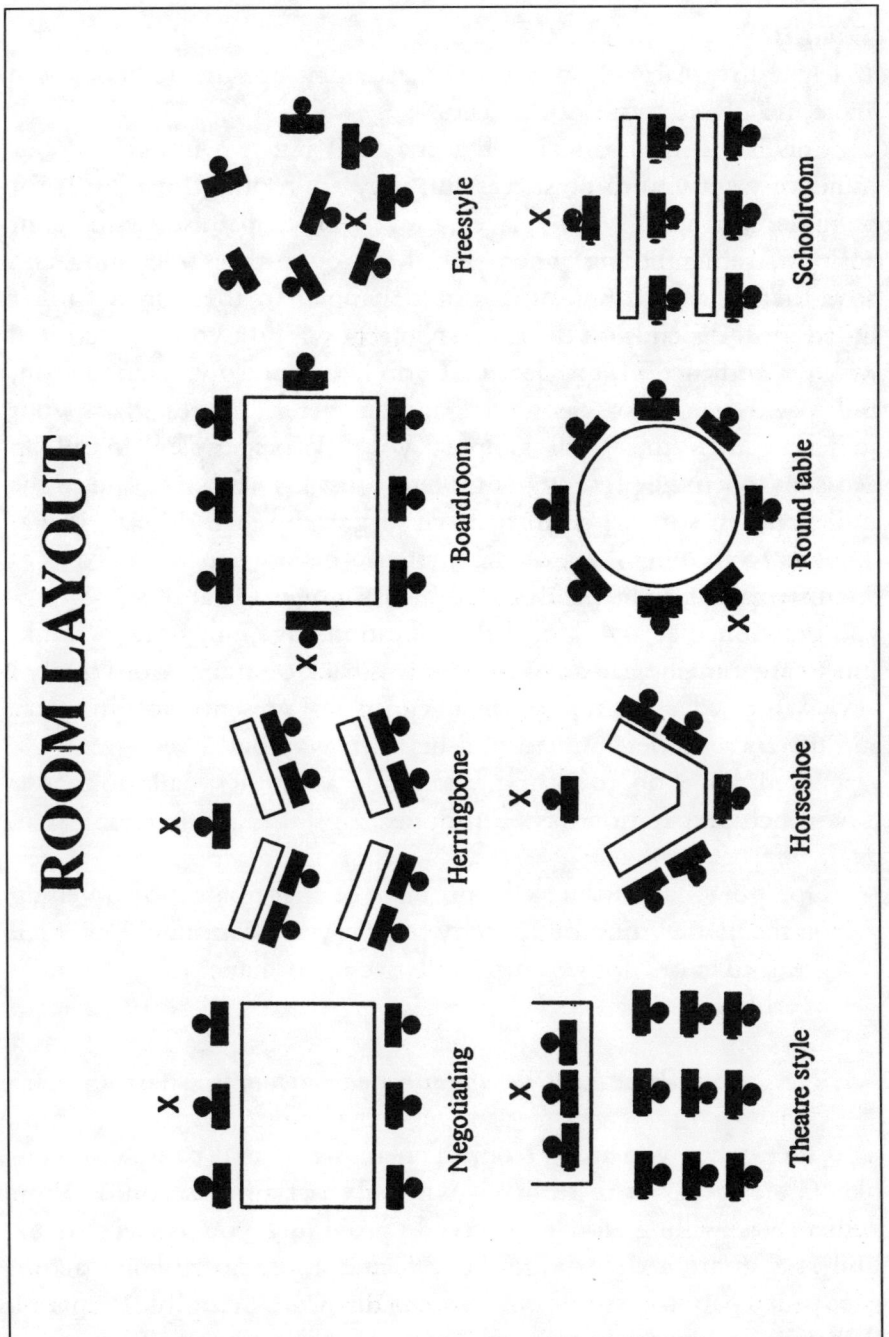

'What if?'
'If I lose my place, drop my overhead, dry up, the audience will make fun of me, walk out . . . etc.'

This is a common fear. They may do, but it is unlikely. Your audience want you to be successful, they are rooting for you. If for example you lose your place, they will empathise with your position, remembering when they have done the same thing and how they felt, or thinking it could happen to them in a similar situation. It depends on the atmosphere of warmth you have created with the audience. If it is clear that you have done your preparation, and you come across as a pleasant character, interested in your audience, then they will support you. For example I recall an occasion when the presenter completely lost his place. He said to the audience 'I'm sorry, I seem to have forgotten where I was'. It was obvious to the members of the audience he was stuck, and one of them stepped in to help. 'Bill, could I ask a question at this point . . . you mentioned . . .' Asking Bill a question gave him time to think, and by the time he had answered he was back on track. Conversely I have witnessed a situation when an egotistical presenter lost his place and the audience left him to find his own way out!

When things do go wrong, and on occasion they will, no matter how much preparation has been done:

- Don't draw attention to the problem or exacerbate it by dwelling on the matter, aim for a speedy recovery and continue. Don't tell the audience, for example, 'I seem to have lost the next overhead'.

Pause – recover the situation – continue

Often when you are in front of an audience, that pause can seem like an eternity, but in reality it will only last a few seconds. Your audience is willing you to succeed, providing you respect them. Unless you are a right-wing Tory facing a Labour militant action group, it's safe to assume that your audience is friendly. Prepare a 'What If' list as part of your preparation. Ask yourself 'What if . . .

INITIAL PREPARATION

for example, the bulb on the overhead blows?' Make contingency plans for all equipment, materials, etc. An equipment list might include things like spare projector bulb, extension lead, plug, screwdriver. Materials: spare pens, masking tape, pre-prepared flipchart.

With good preparation you will reduce the risk of things going wrong. If they do (and on occasion this will be out of your control) you will at least be prepared with a contingency plan.

WHAT IF?

	CONTINGENCY
1. Personal	
2. Material	
3. Equipment	
4. Venue	
5. Other	

4. Impact

Formulate Your Approach
Having determined that you need to communicate and that the presentation is feasible, you are now ready to develop the ideas for the presentation.

Organisation of your communication is an important element, since the way you put together your ideas determines largely how well you will give and how well your audience will receive your message. An understanding of how ideas are put together is vital to successful presentations.

Structure for the Audience
Before starting ask yourself – What particular idea pattern is likely to hit the objectives when speaking to this particular audience?
We will look at two different approaches, logical and psychological.

Logical Approaches
These are essentially rational and message-oriented. That is, your emphasis is on getting ideas into the brains of your audience without concern for their feelings. Logical approaches are generally overt, clear and direct. This approach is useful in certain presentations which we will discuss later.

Psychological Approaches
These are basically the non rational and feeling oriented approaches. Here the main focus is on handling the members' emotional states so that they are willing to accept and assimilate your message. Psychological approaches are normally covert and indirect.

LOGICAL APPROACHES

As stated these are rational and message-centred and their basic purpose is to convey ideas. In this respect the logical approaches serve two very useful ends: to inform (through instruction, exposition and explanation) and to convince through logical demonstration. In informing, the basic quality required is clarity; in convincing it is logical demonstration. The essential element is truth, put forward by use of reasoning, theories and connections. Since they are generally straightforward and direct, logical approaches are frequently deductive i.e. from the clearly stated general to the equally clearly drawn specific conclusion. Types of logical approach follow later; you will find them useful in helping you put ideas together for informative and demonstration-centred presentations.

Time Structure
This puts ideas in chronological or temporal order. While commonly starting with the earliest event and then moving on to later ones (historical development) it can start from the most recent and work back to the earlier. Sometimes it can start at a midpoint and move successively in both directions from it. Time structure is especially useful in imparting background or process information. Background information is by definition historical.

Space Structure
This places ideas in locational relationships i.e. where things are. It has a variety of uses – orientation of equipment or geographical territories, for example the sales offices of a company. This would set the scene for further explanation of a process.

Key Elements Structure
Another way of logically ordering your ideas. It is the one favoured in textbooks and professional journals.

Problem-Analysis-Solution Structure
This progresses from a statement of the situation (the problem) to why it exists (analysis) and then how to handle it (solution). This is a particularly useful technique in making recommendations, reports and proposals, and in introducing changes in the organisation.

Proposition-Proof-Conclusion
This structure moves from

a) The statement of that which is to be demonstrated e.g. thesis, proposal, to
b) Supporting generalisations, theories which prove it, to
c) Conclusions or implications which logically follow.

This method has a most important application in presenting professional, scientific and managerial ideas.

The above structures are not mutually exclusive; indeed they are used frequently to complement each other, or by using one as the primary and the others as supplementary.

Psychological approach

You will remember from the introduction to this section that these are person rather than idea-related. In other words, the beneath the surface impact of your message on the audience is of prime concern. It is designed to control your audience's feelings so that they are willing to listen and accept your ideas.

This method is particularly useful in persuasive communications (deepening existing attitudes and beliefs, changing neutral or opposing viewpoints, or selling managers on some new idea). While not necessarily illogical, psychological structures serve best in non-logical situations. In other words, they deal with the logic of human feelings rather than ideas.

We said earlier that psychological structures are often inductive – that is, moving from the particular to the specific to the more general. Often the generalisation will not be expounded – leaving the audience to draw their own implications.

Some examples of psychological structure:

The Common To Uncommon
This involves moving from that which is initially acceptable to that which is unacceptable. This is directed towards changing listener beliefs and outlooks. It is especially useful in situations where the audience are initially neutral or opposed to your ideas.

The Familiar to Unfamiliar
This refers, of course, to starting with the known and moving in logical steps to the unknown. We are talking about audience familiarity and unfamiliarity. (This is why it is fundamentally a psychological approach).

Here you build understanding to get them to comprehend the new policies, concepts, procedures, products or services – about which they may feel suspicious or inadequate.

This sequence is particularly useful when you are faced with an audience who feel that they know more than you can tell them.

Brief to Action
This involves moving your audience from mental acceptance to desired performance. This approach builds on the three preceding ones, using combinations of each as required. It is useful when you want to stimulate action from an audience who have been brought to the point of belief.

PUTTING IDEAS TOGETHER

A good sequence, whether logical or psychological, is a most important ingredient of presentation success. But it is also clear that you must effectively build out or develop your basic format if you are to deliver the right communication package.

Essentially, developing ideas means the ways by which you make meaningful, or elaborate or support the more general concepts in the essential sequence. In other words, ideas development imparts vitality or clarity or credibility to the more abstract ideas in your fundamental outline. Presentational quality can be no better than the quality of its idea development.

Let's now look at some of the general supportive means you can use in this very important phase of presentation planning. Later we will study detailed techniques and methods.

Facts and Statistics

Facts are verbal statements of either observed or generalised data. Statistics are quantified data, both observed and generalised. Facts and statistics are widely useful, but have special application to logical sequences.

Examples

These can be either a case situation (a detailed event or incident) or real (short account of an actual happening) or hypothetical (fictional). Examples are powerful means to clarify, explain or dramatise ideas. They are useful in almost any type of presentation. We'll explore even more types and their uses in later chapters.

Comparisons and Contrasts

Although often based on facts and statistics, these develop ideas in unique ways. Comparisons are concerned with similarities and analogies; contrasts refer to dissimilarities.

Stories and Anecdotes

Stories may be humorous (jokes), enigmatic (fables) or moralistic (parables). An anecdote is a narrative story – that is, a brief account of an amusing or curious event or happening. Stories and anecdotes have wide appeal and application.

Literary Devices

These include a wide range, such as metaphor (figurative analogy), hyperbole (literary exaggeration), understatement (literary – low key), satire (lampooning or caricature) paradox (that which goes against common opinion), slogan (catchy capsule of an idea), or a quotation (using the words or ideas of someone else).

Demonstration
Here you show an object or the working of an operation. Therefore it goes beyond any of the preceding developmental means, in that demonstration communicates the nonverbal, the real-world item or process. Demonstration has great impact when properly handled. It is especially valuable in technology and scientific presentation.

Audience Participation
This means getting your listeners involved in some part of the presentation. You may ask your audience to help solve the problem you are presenting; you may use a question and answer follow up; you may put your listeners into discussion groups for further clarification or extension of the ideas you have presented.

Audience participation can be used before, during, and after almost any presentation. Uses, of course, depend on your presentation objectives and the intended impact.

In summary, some general ways to develop your ideas are: facts and statistics, comparisons and contrasts; examples, literary devices; stories and anecdotes, visual aids, demonstrations and audience participation.

INTRODUCTIONS

What is the introduction supposed to do? It can be used to accomplish any of these goals: 1. Informing the audience about the presentation subject or development. 2. Convincing the audience of the important of the situation or subject. 3. Reinforcing audience attitudes and beliefs toward you, the situation or your subject. 4. Setting the stage for some specific action or reaction you want from your audience before, during, or after your presentation. It is possible to use any combination of these, depending on your presentation objective.

Informative Introductions

Pre-summary – a concise listing of the main points you plan to cover; it is your presentation in outline form. Note: Keep it brief and clear.

Background Information – This is a brief outline of relevant data giving rise to the presentation – The what, why, who, when and how. Note: Keep brief, don't overdo it.

Facts and Statistics – Refers to condensed and relevant information which the audience may need to understand your presentation message. Note: Same as background information.

Examples – These include striking cases or real or hypothetical happenings. Often useful in making your audience better understand what is to follow. Note: Use only readily understood and relevant ones.

Quotation – From respected sources – frequently used for ready audience credence. Note: be sure your sources are in fact respected.

Reasoned Facts and Statistics – Those that appear valid and reliable to your audience can often induct ready reception. Note: Construct carefully and concisely in an introduction.

Demonstration – If well done it is a powerful method to get immediate conviction. If botched, it has the opposite effect.

Visual Aids – Also good for convincing the audience for most of the reasons previously mentioned. They are excellent devices for getting and holding audience attention and interest.

Furthermore, the audience are often convinced by for example good slides, by the mere fact that you have taken the time and trouble to prepare them, and see this as evidence of your own concern and conviction. Note: Use visuals only as a means to an end, not as ends in themselves.

Literary Devices – Very good introductory means in reinforcement. Metaphors, slogans, unique language, literary description, are all possible ways to get the needed early impact. Note: Don't over-dramatise or appear affected.

Achievements and Traditions – These can be good historical starters. They refer respectively to success achieved by members of the audience or others whom they respect, and customs and practices to which they subscribe. Note: Avoid flattery. Praise must always be sincere.

Ideas and Goals – The basic values and aspirations of your audience or others whom they admire or respect. Achievements and traditions refer to the past; ideals and goals refer to the present and the future.

References to existing audience values or their aspirations are often excellent ways to reinforce attitudes and beliefs. Note: Avoid platitudes and clichés.

Action Introduction – Any of the devices discussed under information, conviction or reinforcing may suit your purpose.

Other possibilities are:

Direct Statement – This means starting your presentation by telling your listeners what performance you want. Note: Avoid this introduction with hostile audiences.

Posing the Problem – A direct or indirect setting forth of the trouble or condition about which you are going to communicate. This can be used when you want to move your listeners to think actively with you as you present subsequent analysis and possible solutions to the problem. Note: Best used with critically oriented audiences.

Audience Participation – Is in itself a form of action whether asking for a show of hands, or asking questions to collect data. Audience participation is both a means and an end to action. Note: Keep it to a minimum, or it may end up like a schoolroom situation.

Creating Suspense – This is another method of action-centred introduction. Here you start your presentation by making your audience uncertain about outcomes or where you are going. In so doing they must actively listen to find out. Note: Don't create apathy or hostility by overdoing.

CONCLUSIONS

Let's now look at some of the ways of ending your presentations. Since conclusions can serve the same essential purposes as introductions, i.e. convincing, informing, reinforcing or action, we shall consider them under the same headings – informative, convincing, reinforcing or action conclusions.

Informative conclusions

Reprisal – This is the final summing up of your ideas. 'The first point was ... the second point was ...' or by succinct paraphrasing of your message. Note: Make it brief, don't give the presentation all over again. Remember key points.

Important Ideas – This is setting out only the most important idea or ideas you want your listeners to remember (key points) leaving out the rest. Note: Don't use with critically minded group, or they may ask –Why did he give us all that information, just to tell us this?

Implications and Inferences – Here you point out where your ideas lead, what they mean, what 'therefores' follow. This is especially useful for critical receivers. Note: Check that your 'therefores' are clear.

Clarifying Examples – Also useful to bring abstract ideas down to earth and make them more meaningful. Note: Could be a danger that the example will be remembered to the exclusion of the basic idea it exemplifies.

Convincing conclusions

Striking Examples – Often as applicable as in introductions. In conclusions they induce credibility by driving home, by vivifying, or by making your ideas more real. Note: Check that your examples strike the right chord – neither over nor underdone, or your whole presentation may become ineffectual.

Quotations – Can also be used in endings. Testimony which restates or supports your thesis or points to some important implication is often a fruitful way to conclude with conviction. Note: Use only relevant quotations.

Demonstration – Is, again, another device equally useful in introductions and conclusions. In conclusions, effective demonstration can put seal on credibility, a good example of ending on a high. Note: Preparation is the key: double-check all equipment, have a contingency plan.

Visuals – Useful device. Visuals can help to reinforce graphically, for example, key points to remember.

All the devices discussed under reinforcing introductions apply equally to reinforcing conclusions.

Additions:
Dramatic Details – Refer to a climactic ordering of ideas, a cumulative effect – ending in a climax. Note: Sincerity is important here, avoid theatrics, unless the situation calls for this.

Visionary – These are endings which predict what can be: for example, a world without pollution, or a doubling of employee salaries within the next five years. Visionary here doesn't mean Utopian, but rather foreseeing realistic outcomes.

The Imaginative – This is where you paint a scenario. For example – picture this – a paperless office. Note: Avoid appearing to exaggerate.

Overcoming Diversity – Is the conclusion in which you point the way for the audience to overcome adversity or conditions. It is especially useful and appropriate in times of distress or agony, in situations where the members of the audience need reinforcement in order to rise above their immediate anguish and look to the future. Note: Use only for situations similar to the above.

Challenge – This means throwing down the gauntlet to the audience – to do what is needed. This can be either subtle or direct. Note: Prepare your audience so that they are ready for this approach.

Plan for Action – Spells out the who, what, when, and how to be done. Especially good for introducing new policies or procedures.

Appeal for Help – Asking your audience to help solve common difficulties or problems.

1. Seeking their cooperation
2. Asking for suggestions and support

Note: This works most effectively when the audience understand what's in it for them (benefits of helping).

Some presenters like to work on their close of the presentation before any other area and then work backwards. Whichever way you decide to tackle it, the ending should be brief and bold.

Your closing remarks are your last chance to convey the message, so recap your main points (reprise). Avoid such anticlimactic closes 'as thank you very much'. However, if you have enjoyed the experience, or have had a particularly enthusiastic or participative audience, you may wish to pay them a compliment, but always be sincere.

Try to end on a positive note – a high. Once you have built up to the climax, stop – sit down.

Support your Ideas

Support material can make the simplest, most ordinary talk interesting. Presenters who produce interesting support material to clarify and prove their main ideas sound more authentic and lively.

Bear in mind that your presentation will only be as interesting as its supporting material. Use facts, cases and illustrations to clarify and, with the use of reasoning, prove your points.

Visual Aids

We will deal with these later, but at this stage plan to use them to help you connect and link ideas together. One of the questions I am often asked is 'are visual aids necessary?' In nine presentations out of ten visuals can add something to the presentation. The exception is the motivational speech, where visuals would be an intrusion.

Some years ago researchers into memory looked at particular types of communication and their effect on information recall.

A survey of people's capability to recall information given to them under controlled conditions showed the following:

Communication Method	Recall Period	
	After 3 Hours	After 3 Days
TELL	70%	10%
SHOW	72%	20%
TELL & SHOW	85%	65%

Remember – *ALWAYS* support your presentation visually.

Make it Punchy
Another way of holding audience attention is to vary the way that you present the information. For example, use the following format when:

Presenting Information
Major idea – detail – detail – recap

Bad News or to Persuade
Hint – detail – detail – detail – major idea – recap

To present Ideas to Management
Use the mnemonic: preface, position, problem, possibility, proposal, postscript. If what you propose has a drawback, present it in the first half of your sentence, and then present the benefits which will trade that off. Always put the limitation first.

Power
Begin powerfully. Everything about you should come across as being positive, including your stand and your voice. Let your enthusiasm show. Let your audience see how happy you are to be talking to them. Communicate with your audience, don't lecture them. Involve them as soon as possible.

Maximise Involvement
Ask rhetorical questions to increase audience interest. This is another good way of presenting information in a different way.

Repeat
Your audience will be better able to remember points that you repeat regularly. Commercial advertisers are expert in this technique. Whether it is a statistic, product name, or any other relevant information which you want the audience to remember, repeat it and give the audience time to digest the importance of the information.

Emphasise
Stimulate your audience; present the facts in a variety of ways which will help them remember the key points.

IMPACT AND DEVICES

Desired Impact	*Devices*
Attention/Interest (apathy)	The shocking or the novel Humour The familiar The Inside Story Directness or animation Stories and anecdotes Demonstration Audiovisuals Audience participation
New perspective (sophistication)	Building audience respect Face validity 'As you know' Metaphor and hyperbole Quotations from respected persons and sources
Eliminating or abating opposition (hostility)	Common ground Starting with common values or beliefs Using respected sources or people Commendations for achievements and tradition Placing disagreement in the broader context of agreement Case examples Candour

	Compromise
	Laying it on the line
	Gaining audience respect
	Admission by wrongdoing
Dramatising (credence)	Heart-rending story
	Heart-interesting story
	Telling details
	Appeal to authority
	Conflict or dramatic event
	Literary devices
	'We shall overcome'
	Dramatic details
	Great ideals or goals
Validation/scrutiny (critical)	Stating basic assumptions and premises
	Stating purposes, thesis and hypothesis
	Stating viewpoint, scope and limitations
	Stating procedures and methods
	Stating conclusions or implications
	Stating gaps or weaknesses
	Providing for criticism
	Modifying or communicating

Summary of Introductions

Objectives	Devices	Cautions
1) Informing	Pre-summary	Be brief and clear
	Background Information	Avoid audience apathy
	Facts and statistics	Avoid audience apathy
	Examples	Use understandable and relevant ones

2) Convincing	Striking examples	Avoid possibly offensive ones
	Quotations from respected sources	Be sure of audience respect
	Researched facts and Statistics	Package carefully and concisely
	Demonstration	Be sure it will work right
	Audiovisuals	Use as a means, not an end
3) Reinforcing	Stories	Make succinct and relevant
	Literary devices	Avoid overdramatics and affectation
	Achievements and traditions	Avoid appearance of flattery
	Great ideals and goals	Avoid platitudes and clichés
4) Action	Direct statement	Do not use with hostile or sophisticated receivers
	Posing the problem	Best used with critical receivers
	Receiver participation	Avoid overdoing
	Creating suspense	Avoid creating apathy or hostility

SUMMARY OF CONCLUSIONS

Objectives	*Devices*	*Cautions*
1) Informing	Post-summary	Make it brief and to the point

	Important ideas	Avoid with critical listeners
	Implications and inferences	Make conclusions clear and proper
	Clarifying examples	Emphasise relation to basic ideas
2) Convincing	Striking examples	Avoid overdoing or underdoing
	Quotations	Use relevant and credible ones
	Demonstration	Be sure it works; emphasise relation to ideas
	Audiovisuals	Avoid obliterating or de-emphasising ideas
3) Reinforcing	All devices listed in Introductions plus:	Same as in introductions
	Dramatic details	Avoid theatrics; be sincere
	Visionary outcomes	Avoid exaggeration
	We shall overcome	Use only in adverse or distressing conditions
4) Action	All devices listed in Introductions plus:	Same as in introductions
	Challenge	Be sure of audience readiness
	Plan for action	Give highlights orally; give details in writing
	Appeal for help	Emphasise receiver benefits

5. Effective Communication

When you speak to an audience, many factors combine to convey a message about you. They include your posture, your gestures, your clothes, your accent, your reputation and many more. These factors should not work in opposition to your message, but should positively reinforce it. Lack of preparation and thought about the small detail may set up barriers to effective communication.

We looked earlier at some checks you should make with regard to the room layout and facilities. These areas all form part of your professionalism. If the seating arrangements, for example, are inappropriate for the size of the group, or you allow delegates to smoke in a poorly ventilated room, they will blame you. You are in control of the situation and must be responsible.

The majority of the audience will appreciate you being assertive, if you are polite.

Smoking
For example, if asking a group not to smoke, after the preliminaries I would normally say 'I would appreciate it if we have no smoking during the presentation. We'll be moving next door for coffee in about 30 minutes, and you can smoke then.' I would probably also say 'Does everyone agree?' I have never had anyone disagree with this suggestion, particularly as smokers now seem to be in the minority.

Seating

You may find that you are speaking in a large room and most of the audience are scattered towards the back. This can happen for example:

a) If you have to speak in a lecture theatre. If it doesn't have a capacity audience, what tends to happen is that the audience fill it up from the back, with a few brave people coming down front to sit. Also, if it is three-sided, one side may be favoured over another.
b) When you are speaking late in the day after many of the audience have left, leaving the remainder sprinkled around the theatre.

Again, be polite and ask them to come down to the front (gesture towards where you want them to go). Give them a minute or so to regroup before you begin.

Environment

If the audience are physically unable to see and hear properly due to environmental factors they will switch off.

Some examples of this are external traffic noise, noisy air conditioning, poor lighting, wrong layout for size of room and audience, room temperature too hot or cold. Frequent interruptions, e.g. telephone ringing. I was once speaking in a hotel and took the precaution of checking out the meeting room beforehand. It seemed ideal, and satisfied my checklist of requirements. However, on the day, I discovered that the room was right next to the hotel kitchens, and I had to compete with chef's orders and crashing crockery. A colleague had a similar experience in an Edinburgh hotel, when half-way through his pitch the air was filled with strains of the Skye Boat Song – played on the bagpipes!

It is always wise to ask if the adjoining room is being used.

Sometimes the audience are unable to concentrate when they cannot see the relevance of the subject. They may feel that it has no interest or significance to them. Alternatively, the language used may not be understood, or the presenter may be giving mixed messages.

Emotions, prejudices, assumptions can cloud the intended message, because people attend the presentation with their own views on the subject being presented.

Take the following steps:

- Always begin by correctly identifying with the needs of your audience, i.e. what are their objectives, and do they match mine?
- Ask questions to establish information
- Sell them the benefits which will satisfy their needs
- Demonstrate how these benefits will be delivered
- Appeal to their values and aspirations. If what you say goes against their beliefs, they will resist. Relate to them as individuals.

Language

Often people worry that their accent is not acceptable to others. In most cases this is untrue. Like your handwriting and your fingerprints, your accent in unique to you, and as such is part of your personality.

Most members of the audience welcome a different, or unusual accent. Some accents add a touch of charm and individuality – think of the French accent.

Often an accent will help the audience listen more attentively to make sure they do not miss anything.

N.B. This assumes that the accent does not get in the way of communication, i.e. that diction and enunciation remain clear. In all the time I have given and attended presentations, I have never had negative complaints from the audience about accent. Any comments have always been positive and are usually a precursor to further communication.

Practise speaking clearly and crisply. You can be proud of your accent, providing your audience can clearly understand what you are saying.

If you are speaking to foreign groups there are a few additional points to bear in mind.

Another barrier to effective communication may be self-induced: the effects of alcohol.

Alcohol mixed with the stimulation of excitement can be a lethal mixture. You no doubt know your capacity for alcohol and this is one occasion where you should be careful. If you are speaking after lunch or dinner, where the drink is flowing freely, either abstain completely, and opt for soda on the rocks or mineral water, or have only as much wine as will produce a warm glow and no more. Many people feel that a glass of wine relaxes them and if so that's fine, but have no more than you need to loosen up a little. (Beware of the over-solicitous wine waiter who refills the glass.) It is so easy to drink more than you intended, and often the result is not apparent until you fluff a line or lose your place.

Drink is like success: both are terrific until they go to your head.

Uses of Written Presentation Documents

In relation to presentation skills, written media may be viewed as 'printed hardware'. Although we are emphasising oral communication, writing also plays an important role in many managerial and professional presentations. For example, papers are read aloud word for word to colleagues at professional meetings. In this case, the written material is primary, and the oral merely verbal reinforcement. Alternatively, in order to help employees remember accurately what he said at the weekly staff meeting, the head of the department may send a written summary as a follow-up. The following is a selection of written media used in conjunction with presentations. Used correctly they will help easy effective communication with your group.

Letters and Memoranda

Letters and memoranda are useful to:

- Arrange for a presentation (notifying time, place, agenda)
- Follow up after the presentation (summary, 'for the record' communication, request for action, notification of further presentations)

- Use as testimonial communication (specimen letters of complaint, examples of poor company letters to customers)
- Vitalise the oral presentation (communicating importance, pointing out potential benefits)

Reports
Reports can be used to:

- Document or support ideas in the oral presentation
- Focus discussion on some specific aspect, such as falling sales or production discrepancies
- Act as an outline guide for oral presentation (discussing a production report item by item, or pointing out where improvements are needed in accuracy and validity of certain reported data
- Present important conclusions from meetings, conferences, or exploratory communications
- As the essential presentation itself, whether extemporised or read aloud *verbatim*

Proposals
These put forth ideas for consideration, generally for the purpose of decision or action (for example, plans for redesign of the company's distribution centre or a bid for the sale of some product or service). They are frequently employed:

- As the essential basis of the presentation (for example, a consultancy group spelling out the what, when, where and how of a bid to representatives of the Department of the Environment)
- As a result of prior oral presentation or discussion, such as a manager asking his staff to come up with a plan for better time management discussed in a staff meeting
- As the definitive spelling out of more general orally presented ideas (for example an oral presentation of the company's

departmental relocation, followed by a detailed step-by-step written scheme)

Directives
As guides for action, these can be used to:

- Authenticate oral presentation on policy or procedural interpretation (such as to clarify what an existing policy means and why, or to sanction a new procedure)
- Help introduce a policy or procedural change (for example a different basis for providing childcare facilities)
- Help reinforce interpretations and actions called for (such as to remind people of a policy's existence or to renew understanding of how things are to be done)
- Be the central focus for a presentation (where item-by-item oral analysis and interpretation of the directive is needed)

Agreements and Commitments
Agreements are written dialogues between two or more parties i.e. they are bilateral or multilateral. Commitments, on the other hand, are essentially unilateral. Agreements may be intracompany, such as write-ups of different departmental responsibilities in carrying out a cost-cutting programme, or intercompany, such as understandings between the company and various suppliers about delivery schedules and payment procedures. Commitments bind the originator to provide a particular service to the receiver (such as a contract to build a new computer centre at a given price, within a certain time following explicit specifications).

Both agreements and commitments tend to technical rigor, specificity and detail, all necessary so that all parties know exactly to what they agree or are committed.

Where are written agreements and commitments useful in presentation?

- As bases for clarification and interpretation (e.g. the exact meaning of contract details)

- As supporting documents in more broadly based presentations
- As written follow-ups to prior oral agreements or commitments

Manuals

These are directives or guides to actions for specific groups, such as clerical workers, supervisors. Generally they are published in loose-leaf or bound format for continuing guidance. Manuals are often the most important job-related documents in an organisation. As such, they can be used in presentations to:

- Renew understanding of small or large segments of task oriented information
- Introduce new ways of doing things
- Get feedback on operators' understanding of existing instructions
- Get suggestions for improvements in methods and procedures

In-House Communications

These include informal company newsletters, newspapers, magazines. This type of communication is often management's principal means of communication with employees.

They supplement the oral presentation in the following ways:

- As announcements for meetings, conferences, seminars
- As means for communicating the importance of forthcoming presentations
- As ways to solicit ideas, suggestions, complaints, which could lead to a presentation
- As testimonials in presentations, such as quoting the chairman's remarks on the importance of corporate responsibility or a letter to the editor from an employee complaining about holiday entitlement
- As follow-ups to presentations, reinforcement of key ideas, requests for specific related actions or decisions

Company Brochures

These are formal written packages for specific receiver groups such as shareholders, customers or employees. Examples are annual reports, new product write-ups, or booklets on company benefits. They carry specific messages to selected target readers.

They can be effectively employed as supplements in oral presentations:

- As principal bases for the communication, whether sent before, or given out during the presentation
- As 'teasers' to get attention and interest, either before or during the presentation
- As detailed explanations of ideas highlighted in oral presentations
- As audience control devices during the presentation, for example directing listeners to specific points at intervals or to help answer questions raised during or after the presentation
- As follow-ups for the listeners or for dissemination to an even broader target group (for example, sending the president's annual address to company managers in similar industries).

Professional Papers

Common in managerial, professional and scientific circles, these are critically oriented written communications concerning importance problems, theories, concepts, methodologies, and research findings. With this kind of communication medium, the written document is of prime importance; the oral reading of the paper serves only to highlight or emphasise ideas. The paper can also be the focus of subsequent critiques.

Functions of the professional paper include the following:

- They are the basic presentation for situations where serious management professional or scientific ideas are to be communicated
- They can be published for wider distribution e.g. in professional journals

- They can be sent to colleagues for technical critique or review, either before or after the presentation
- They can be sent to a larger body of potentially interested professionals for their information
- They can be 'popularized' for mass distribution to nonprofessionals (for example newspaper and trade journals)

We have listed the types and uses of presentation documents. Let's now look at each subject in turn.

Letters and Memoranda
The purposes of letters are many and varied, ranging from simple and direct to very complex and subtle. The essential emphasis, however, is personalisation – i.e. they are addressed to specific people in specific situations. Letters are generally addressed to people outside the organisation, while memoranda are most often in-house.

To obtain the desired personal impact, keep these principles in mind:

1. Know your reader, who, what, when and why.
2. Make the reader feel you are communicating with him and not to him.
3. Use the reader's language level, which is not necessarily yours.
4. Communicate in terms of the reader's understanding of the subject.
5. Communicate the right company image.
6. Be as formal or informal as the situation dictates, keeping in mind your objectives.
7. Use to set the stage, follow up, or support the oral presentation – as the situation dictates.

Reports
A report is written in response to some specific request, whether routine or special. Therefore the purpose of a given report is spelled out in its requirements and attendant instructions. Like letters and memoranda, reports also originate from some identified person and

are addressed to some named person or people. To make reports communicative and helpful in your presentation, you should remember these guidelines:

1. Know exactly what the report calls for, from its instructions.
2. Be sure that you cover all the information called for, as best you can.
3. If certain information cannot be supplied, state the reasons, and when you'll supply the missing data.
4. Follow exactly the format and style called for (if these are not given, create appropriate ones).
5. In oral presentations, visual devices such as overhead transparencies can be used to supplement the conventional report, to keep listener attention and interest.

Proposals

Since these focus on getting favourable decision or action about some idea, plan or scheme, and since proposals are frequently the presentation itself, you should keep the following in mind:

1. Know exactly the proposal's mission – whether it is a decision or an action, and specifically what decision or action.
2. Select and include only those data to meet the mission – including both descriptive and evaluative data.
3. Build your (or other proposer's) competence and credibility to carry out the proposal's objectives.
4. Clearly state your method of implementing your plan or scheme – what, when, where and how.
5. Address the proposal to a person or position with sanction to approve.
6. In presentations, highlight orally; spell out details in writing.
7. Use preparatory and summary materials (sending out before presentation) backup (during presentation), or follow-up (after the presentation).
8. Use visual aids to get better understanding and to help induce conviction.

Directives

Like letters and reports, directives also originate from specific people and go to specific people. As guides to operational activities, however, they have a more impersonal appearance. Clarity and explicitness are necessary for directives. To make them communicate accordingly, bear in mind these guides in using directives with presentation:

1. Know the people you are addressing (use your checklist).
2. Know exactly what must be said to assure the right operational outcomes – and say nothing else.
3. Authenticate the directive (that is, your aim and the company's authoritative basis for issuing).
4. Supplement as needed with other communications, both written and oral.
5. In oral presentations, written handouts, complete, or extracts (copies of overheads), together with visual aids are helpful.
6. Send out directives before or after, or give them out during the oral presentation (as appropriate to achieve your objectives).

Agreements and Commitments

Essentially 'contractural' , agreements and commitments must be explicit and clear as to what is expected of all parties involved. These are guides to presentational effectiveness:

1. Set out the exact requirements to be met, tasks, times and cost.
2. Set out the specific parties involved: names, position, companies.
3. Set out 'penalties' or other means of satisfaction if any party fails in his assigned role (or if no penalties, say so).
4. Get oral agreement first, followed by detailed written documents (which should also be thoroughly discussed to assure complete understanding of all parties).
5. Use before, during, or after the presentation proper depending on indicated need.

Manuals

As broad guides to action, these are addressed to as wide a reader spectrum as possible, commensurate with assuring proper job performance. For example, in many organisations a manual can be written for administrative staff, or company personnel, regardless of their location. However, care must be taken to get proper understanding and acceptance of the document. Therefore, differentiation within the firm is frequently necessary (for instance, between sales manuals and machine operator manuals). With these in mind, here are some guides to make manuals communicative in presentations:

1. Use language and graphics which can be understood by everybody in the relevant group – e.g. (sales staff, personnel groups, marketing managers).
2. Use 'persuasive instruction' where possible to assure acceptance by readers.
3. Make the manual attractive in appearance, format and company style, so that it appeals to the reader.
4. Make the manual flexible so that it can be updated, for instance in loose-leaf binding.
5. Get continuing user feedback so that improvements can be made.
6. In oral presentation before, during or after as needed (whether as the central focus or as backup).
7. Use visual aids to reinforce ideas and help induce conviction and action.
8. Always provide an opportunity for receivers to give reactions, raise questions, or seek interpretations during or after the presentation – so that optimal understanding can be gained from the exchange of ideas.

Forms

These are usually tightly structured and styled media for gathering, reporting and storing information. As such, they must both suit the organisation's informal purpose and get user acceptance. Here are some suggestions for construction and use in presentations:

1. Make the form both complete and attractive – including instructions for use.
2. Address the form to a specific target purpose (remember 'smart' objectives).
3. Optimise costs (time, money, human resources), in the numbers and types of forms used (eliminating, combining, or adding as appropriate).
4. Make the form communicate clearly and cogently with users, in content, format, language, style, and ease of handling.
5. Set out clearly the processing and flow of the form (origin, destination, storage).
6. In presentations, use for clarification, analysis, backup, emphasis or action.
7. If it is the presentational focus, use slides or overheads (check legibility), to reinforce ideas and induce conviction.
8. In presentations and other occasions, solicit user feedback – essential for further design improvement.

In-House Communications

In-house, broad spectrum, written media should communicate effectively with almost all members of the organisation. Generally mass distributed, they are directed to both organisational and individual needs. Here are some general suggestions for communicability and presentational use:

1. Use appropriate format and style (for the majority of receivers)
2. Make the house communication appear to serve the reader's social or individual needs, with the organisational needs secondary.
3. Use plenty of pictures, charts and items of personal interest.
4. Make appearance optimally attractive, neither too slick nor too amateurish.

5. With presentations, use for announcing and follow-up (when and where, what was said, what it means, and so on).
6. Use as testimonials or backup in presentations, for example indicating problem areas, needs to be met, and so forth.

Brochures
As carriers of information to particular target groups, both inside and outside the company, brochures should be composed and used in these ways:

1. Know the specific target groups for which they are intended (for instance, customers, suppliers, stockholders).
2. Know the exact message which is to be communicated – services offered, specification to be met.
3. Communicate to hit the target group with maximum message impact.
4. Optimise costs – combining, eliminating, or adding brochures to communicate with all major target groups.
5. In presentations, use as handouts (before, during or after).
6. Use in conjunction with the presentation to reinforce, elaborate, induce conviction, or get action (planning and executing your communication accordingly).
7. Use to follow up the presentation (mailing, displaying, distributing through departmental channels).

Professional Papers
As we have seen, these carry critical-based messages about significant ideas, issues, problems or actions in managerial, professional and scientific circles. And, as noted, the professional paper is often the primary presentation vehicle for such occasions. It serves as a common, objective reference for analysis, review, critique and if needed, modification.

In addition to the basic conventional requirements for technical validity, proper reasoning, and appropriate format, you should bear in mind these suggestions for presentation of professional papers.

1. Present your paper to several representative, competent, candid colleagues, and rewrite if their feedback indicates the need (otherwise your invite failure).
2. Send out copies of your final draft to your prospective listeners before the presentation (if this is feasible).
3. Invite written reactions and criticism before you give your presentation, so that you can make any necessary final revisions and also to allow you to prepare answers to anticipated questions.
4. Present your paper aloud in an objective, but communicative manner i.e. keep the critical view, but remember you are addressing human beings whose attention and interest must be sustained.
5. Always allow plenty of time for questions, reactions, comments, which are the real core for testing your ideas.
6. Invite follow-up reactions from your auditors, (i.e. ask them to call or talk with you – or, even better, to write up their thoughts after thinking through your ideas).
7. If you see the need, rewrite the paper after inputs of the kind described in 5 and 6 – and for your own rethinking of your presentation.
8. Distribute or publish the paper as appropriate, assuming of course, that this is desirable and feasible.
9. In the oral presentation, audio visuals are often helpful to clarify ideas and focus attention, but be careful not to create antagonism by appearing to 'put on a show' to a critically oriented group.

These are some general guidelines for using written media in presentations. They must be viewed in terms of your audience and what you are trying to achieve. Used correctly, they can add interest, focus, and gravitas to your performance.

6. Notes

The first thing to be said about notes is – keep them simple. The secret is balance; once you are on your feet, you, the audience and the notes should be in balance. Too elaborate a note and you cannot properly hold the attention of the audience. Too scanty a note and you may begin to wander or waffle. The following are some ideas of how to:

- Organise and edit your brainstorming ideas
- Draft and script
- Decide between script and cards

There is no one successful method. For example don't immediately dismiss the use of cards because you have witnessed them being used badly. Some of the most experienced and celebrated speakers use cards in their performance. In my training courses I encourage managers to experiment with cards. Some try them, and just don't feel happy, and revert to full scripts. Others find cards more manageable and embrace them with enthusiasm. Whatever method you choose, the following information will help you decide what is right for you, in relation to your presentation needs.

Organise and Edit your Ideas
Earlier, we looked at the idea of brainstorming, and I showed you an example using my theme of graphology. One of the problems when deciding what to include in a presentation is that our passion and knowledge of the subject take over. *Everything* about the subject is interesting to us, and we want to tell the audience everything we know.

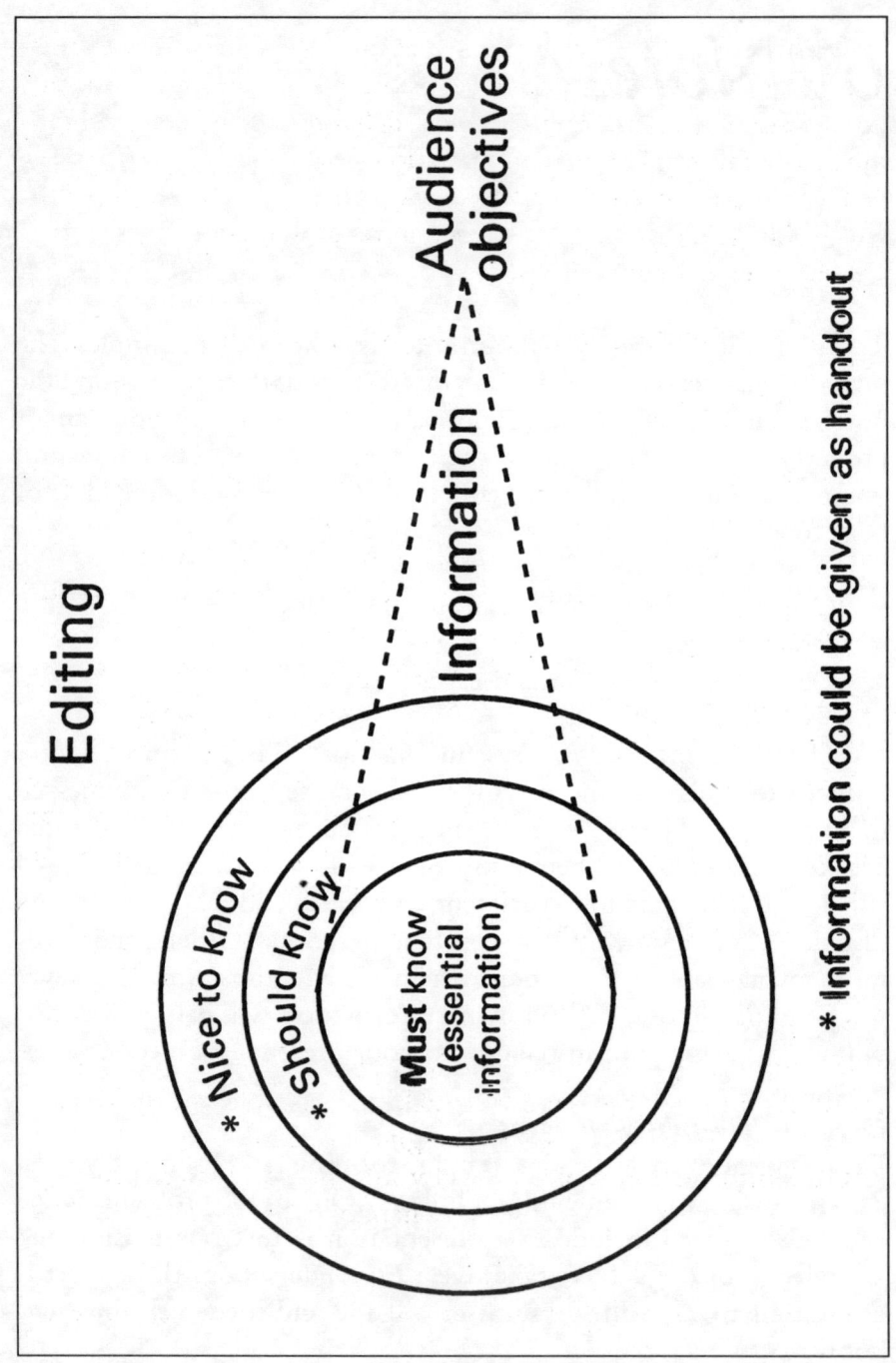

Many potentially excellent presentations have fallen down in this area: clear objectives, good preparation; interesting content; knowledgeable presenter; enthusiastic delivery . . . but far, far too much material in relation to presentation time available.

Therefore I have further edited my graphology example down to manageable proportions for my 30 minute presentation.

Here is how I edited my ideas:

Bear in mind: The time you have available to present
Your objectives
Audience objectives

Then look through the brainstorm notes you made during the initial preparation. Consider your ideas one at a time and ask yourself, 'If I include this information, will it take me towards the objectives?'

In other words, do the audience need to know this information? If so, it must be included. This is often referred to as the 'must know' rule. You can see from the simple chart opposite that this information forms the basis of your presentation. If after, reading through your initial selection, and doing a rough timing, you find that you will have time to spare, you could then include some of the 'should' and 'could' information. This is supplementary material, for example additional support items, such as further examples or statistics, which are not essential to fulfil the objectives, but are relevant to the overall topic.

In Summary
MUST information = essential to fulfil objectives
SHOULD information = not essential, but valuable information.
(Could be given as handouts)
COULD information = nice to know information (fringe benefit)
– include as handouts.

From my graphology brainstorm exercise, an example of each would be:

Edited Ideas
                Subject: Graphology

Handwriting   **Brainwriting (M)**   Training   Saudek   **Michon (M)**

Personality (M)   Health   **Jung (M)**   Illness   Compatibility

Sex   Pulver   Statistics   **Europe (M**)   USA

German/French Schools   Rhythm   Size   Crepieux   Jamin   Klages

Zones (M)   **Business Applications (M)**   Capital Letters   Signatures

Stroke   General Impression   Spacing   Speed   Slant

Examples (M)   **Recruitment (M)**   Crime   Pressure

After highlighting my key MUST information, I would repeat the process for valuable material and fringe material (time allowing).

MUST –   Graphology is a science with a legitimate and important role in character and personality assessment within psychiatry and psychotherapy, personnel management and job evaluation. (Essential information for this particular audience.)

SHOULD –   Scientific graphology has been long recognised in Europe and America. (Valuable background information, but could be given in handout along with some statistics.)

COULD –   Although graphology can reveal character and motivation of a killer, there is no such thing as 'a murderer's handwriting'. (This may, or may not, be a relief to personnel managers, but it would not be appropriate to our objectives in this case.)

However, this last is an interesting branch of graphology, and a little information given about it establishes the scope of the subject and could also provide the basis for another talk. Instead of discounting the information completely, you might consider giving some brief information in a handout . . .

> Just as fingerprints studied by an expert can reveal the identity of a suspect, handwriting, when analysed by an experienced graphologist, can provide unmistakable clues in detecting criminal tendencies. Handwriting and fingerprints are both unique to the owner, but it has taken the judiciary in Britain longer to accept the value of graphology as evidence than it has in Europe. Scotland Yard and the CID in other police forces will consider any leads when painstakingly sifting clues in tracking down criminals, but rarely do they acknowledge publicly that they employ graphologists, preferring to call them handwriting experts. The use of graphology by criminologists . . .

A few examples could then be given . . . for example, the case of the Yorkshire Ripper.

Work Up Your Script
Having decided what information you want to include in the presentation, you can now proceed to shape it.

Step 1
Decide the format. I have decided to divide my talk into three areas; you will find that when you brainstorm your ideas, many will fall 'naturally' under certain sub-headings. Breaking up the material will tell you how much material you have time for.

Remember that the average speaker achieves about 120–150 words per minute. The average attention span of an audience is less than 30 minutes. After about 20 minutes the attention level gradually decreases, so you will need to find ways of 'refreshing' them.

I have broken up my subject into three main areas:

- The history of graphology (background information)
- Basic principles
- Benefits to personnel

and I have decided to cover three key points in each section.

Now that I have decided what key points I want to cover, I can use this information to make up my agenda. For example, the following could be written up on a flipchart if speaking to a small informal group, or alternatively, on an overhead or slide.

Graphology as an Aid to Recruitment

The History of Graphology

- Brainwriting
- The founder, Abbe Michon
- The European approach

Principles

- Personality
- Psychology – Jung
- Zones

Recruitment Benefits

- Business applications
- Recruitment – What's in it for you
- Examples – Case study

The advantages of writing it out as an agenda are:

1. It breaks up the material

2. You could use mini-summaries after each section (or take questions).
3. You can use the agenda to recap and conclude your presentation.

This method makes it easier for you to write up your cards. For example you may decide to use one or two cards for each topic.

Example:

History	Margin
Brainwriting • Influences: the writing organ, hand, foot, mouth. • Writing – Diagrams of the unconscious – scientific evidence • Lord Nelson – example	 OHP Slide no. 1

Step 2
Start working on the close. How should you end? What is the final message which will leave your audience as you want them?
Remember your objective: the close must echo what you want to achieve

Step 3
Create your opening (see previous section)

You must secure attention and interest. Make it appropriate. Try to open – from the first word – with something interesting. Pose a question or paint a picture. (Choose one of the suggested opening techniques.)

Avoid opening with a joke. This is for after-dinner speakers. However, a spontaneous, humorous link to something that happened or something said by the person introducing you can form a good bridge into your presentation.

After you have gained attention, tell your audience:

- The key theme of which they will become convinced

(Have a look at the initial preparation section, which includes a suggested list of things you might include in your introduction.)

Choose from this list what is relevant to your presentation. This will vary each time; for example, if you are introduced by the Chairman, he will give some background information about you. As for timing, this may have been set by the chair, so you don't need to repeat this.

*Whatever else you decide to include – **always** tell them your objectives.*

We discussed earlier the structure of the presentation:

- Opening – Body (key points) – Reprise and Close

Concentrate on your close first. At the end of the presentation, what is the message you want ringing in the ears of the audience? Jot this down, then work through the rest of your script. The development, or body, section will consist of your key points. This is the information that you have decided is essential. Brief headings are sufficient here. Think of the links between each point. This will direct the flow of speech, but not interrupt it. When you have noted down what you want to say, start dictating the whole presentation from your notes. Have this drafted.

The next stage is actually to read the presentation out loud from your notes. You will quickly realise that the written word is not always suitable for speech. A good presentation should be delivered in conversational style; so in the final script add the light and shade to the written word for delivery.

When reading your presentation out loud you will have noticed points, words and phrases that need emphasis, and places where you need to pause. Mark these in pencil as you go through it. You may also find words/phrases which looked good in written form, but don't sound right. Use this information to develop your script. Punctuation is important. Use short sentences; however, it will sound flat if all the sentences are short, so vary their length without sacrificing meaning.

When you have gone through your script a few times, and are happy with the flow, you can then start to polish it and decide whether to use notes or cards.

Notes Versus Cards
The following observations may help you to decide which you prefer.

Cards
Postcard size cards are a useful aid:

- Horizontal or vertical format can be used (this is a matter of preference as there are no hard and fast rules)
- Use one side only
- Write each theme/key point on a separate card
- When you have covered the information on the card turn over
- Number each card and leave loose. Alternatively, use a binder ring or treasury tag in one corner. You can then hold or slip your thumb through the ring (this enables the cards to be kept in order)
- Use easy to handle 4 x 6 cards on which the outline is typed vertically. These cards can be held in your hand like a pack of playing cards.

The benefits of using cards far outweigh the disadvantages of the time it takes to prepare and rehearse with them. They are neat and can be handled discreetly; they are also flexible. For instance, if you find yourself running out of time you can skip one or two cards, or summarise each card in a sentence. In case you should have extra time (this happened to me on one occasion when the next speaker was late and I was asked to talk for a further ten minutes) a few extra cards would be useful. This is where some of your 'should' and 'could' material would be appropriate.

Use Cards for After-Dinner Speaking

Half-cards come into their own here – one or several, it does not matter. Either hold them in the palm of the hand and remember to use the arm as a mobile lectern to raise the notes upwards and forwards; or improvise a rest for them. For instance, stand a brandy glass, or better still a port glass, on a couple of cigar boxes. Squeezing the cards to ensure they are not too springy, slip them into the glass. A port glass particularly makes the cards stand very upright. With a little practice, the cards can quite easily be removed. Take a step forward, looking down at the cards; slip the top one up and out firmly as you step back; look up again at the audience. You may even write the notes so that this movement comes at a natural pause. Be sure that the light is the best obtainable (and allowing for this not being perfect, write or type the notes on the large side)

Notes

These are more visible, but hold more information than the cards. Avoid scraps, and numerous pages of notes. Never hold a single piece of paper in your hand. (If you are nervous, shaking paper is more evident.)

- If there are only a few sheets of paper, place a firm card at the back, if you are going to hold them.
- If using a table lectern, number each sheet in the top left hand corner. Display two sheets at once. Practise the smooth move from one sheet to the next. This method allows you to see two pages at a time (and reduces the rustling effect which often accompanies the handling of notes). Use yellow paper for increased clarity.
- Leave sufficient space between points so that you can read the information easily.

Whether you are using cards or notes, make them work for you. Never use material that other people have written, unless it is adapted to your style of delivery and is appropriate to the audience and subject. Avoid slang, jargon, swear words, and also technical language if speaking to a non-technical audience.

General Hints:

- Draw a margin down one side of the page or card and use this to note where, for example, you will show an overhead slide, write on a flipchart or give a handout.
- Use a red pen to underline key words. Make additional red check marks next to ideas that may need emphasis.
- Underline the opening phrase in each paragraph with a highlighter pen.
- Having visual aids is another means of using notes: slides and charts can serve as an outline and information source for you.
- You can pencil notes in flipchart margins or overhead frames without your audience knowing it.

Polish the key phrases and make allowances for the use of your aids. Now you are ready to rehearse using your script.

Hints on Timing
Initially it is difficult to hit your timing accurately. You should by now have edited your script so that you have included all the information necessary.

- At this stage, mark time checks on each page.
- Allocate the elapsed time from the start of the climax of each key point. Do not use actual times, as start time for presentations can run early or late.
- Mark these times on your notes, say every three minutes for a short presentation, or five minutes for a longer one. As you progress through the presentation you can slow down, speed up,

cut or introduce extra items as necessary in order to finish at the exact time.
- Rehearse your presentation until your timing is right.
- Try the rate of speech and readability test at the end of this chapter.

If you are presenting so much material that time really does press, then experience will let you gauge the overall length of the speech by rehearsing only part (just as a writer estimates the length of his script by checking a few pages). Check that you are within the time allowed – by a minute or so – in order to feel relaxed, not having to speak against the clock. Remember that although you are adopting this procedure to conform to the time allotted to you, what you are doing should still be regarded as a full-blooded rehearsal. Make sure that the delivery is satisfactory, that the facts and ideas link in smoothly and that you are being neither verbose, nor long in your sentences.

Script – How Much is Information
Presenters are often unsure when they should use a full script, or when brief notes are more appropriate.

These guidelines, based on experience, may help you decide:

A full script is advisable when:

- The occasion is formal
- The presentation will be recorded
- The material is complex
- The sequence of audio-visual aids requires fixed cues for the projectionist
- The presenter is inexperienced

Brief notes are recommended when:

- The occasion is not too formal
- The presentation will not be recorded
- The material does not demand a full script

- The speaker is relatively experienced

Short headings are adequate when:

- The occasion is informal
- The presentation will not be recorded
- The material is relatively simple
- The speaker is very experienced

Text Layout
Think carefully about this. Whatever method you use your notes must be legible. The following are some recommendations to ensure success:

1) Use large type

A word processor can help you to achieve the type style you require.

2) Limit the number of words per line

Try not to have more than eight or nine words on a line. This will enable you comfortably to 'photograph' mentally roughly a line at a time.

3) Avoid breaking words

Keep words intact. It is far better to carry the whole word to the next line, leaving extra space, than to break the word with a hyphen. Even compound words with a hyphen should be kept on one line.

4) Use wide margins

Side margins should be at least one inch on each side. Top and bottom margins should be closer to an inch and a half. This will give you a lot of 'white space' around your script, making the print stand out more.

5) Line Spacing

You should at least double space each line. This will vary with the type style. For example, if you are using all capital letters, triple-spacing would be better.

6) Sentence Spacing

Make sure that between each full point and the start of a new sentence you have a good separation so that there is a clear break. Normally, this will be two or three spaces. Again, this will vary with type style.

7) Paragraph Spacing

This will also vary with type style. As a general rule, spacing between paragraphs should be wider than your line spacing.

8) Indent Each Paragraph

This will increase the amount of 'white space' on the page, making it easier for you to keep your place and take your time.

9) End each page with a full point

Never carry a sentence from the bottom of one page to the top of the next. Doing so causes needless delivery problems.

10) Start each page with a new paragraph

As no sentences are carried over from page to page, every page starts with a new sentence, which should be indented as a new paragraph.

This will give you a sense of timing for a smooth page transition, as well as additional 'white space'.

11) Avoid long sentences and paragraphs

Long sentences should be shortened to two, or even three, shorter sentences. Long paragraphs should be split into shorter, more easily handled paragraphs. This will reduce the chances of losing your place.

12) One sentence paragraphs

Making a key sentence a separate paragraph helps you give it the emphasis it deserves.

Making Your Script
Suspension points (. . .) can be used in many places instead of commas. This will improve the layout physically by providing more 'white space' which will give you a better sense of time. Underlining key words and phrases can also help you visually. Avoid using slashes (/) to indicate pauses, which may produce a mechanical or unnatural delivery.

Visual Aids and Cues
You should clearly indicate on your script when a visual aid should be displayed and when it should be removed. This is best done in capital letters, underlined and should be placed in the middle of the page . . . not to the side.
    For example:

SLIDE ON

As far as spacing is concerned, the cue instruction should be treated as a paragraph:

SLIDE OFF

Page Numbers
Page numbers can either be centred at the top of the page or placed in one of the two top corners.

Bifocal Lenses
For those with bifocal lenses, it might be easier to limit the printed information to the upper half or two-thirds of the page.

Reading Someone Else's Speech Effectively
As well as giving presentations from your own notes, there may be business situations where you have to read key words inherited from others.

For example:

- A colleague has been taken ill, and asks you to give his speech to the executive committee.
- You must read accurate and precise instructions to company employees in a way that ensures that they all receive the same information simultaneously.
- Reading scripts may be the custom in your company.

Reading from scripts does not make for the most interesting speeches. However, you as the speaker, should never be boring. The following are a few pointers to help you make a speech that is read as lively and interesting as one given from notes.

Practice
Practice is every bit as important with a script as it is when using notes. They take just as much time to rehearse. If you are fortunate enough to have a speech writer, you can probably get by with a couple of practices. As this is a rare occurrence, you will most likely have to adjust the script to suit yourself.

Making Words Interesting
The words in front of you may for example, may be a straight speech or a list of compiled data. You may have to read a report which is

straightforward and not prone to embellishment. The most important factor is belief in the message. Remember your enthusiasm, look and sound as if it is a great pleasure to be addressing your listeners.

Familiarise Yourself With the Material

The objectives of what you are reading must be absolutely clear to you. Write out your objective on a single card. This is essential if you are using a professional writer, as they will work from this. Think of your objective as you work through the script. Read the material through several times, check all pronunciations of difficult words or names. Once you have decided on the correct one, keep to this throughout.

Divide the whole script into logical parts, and look at content. Study the words that are being used, and also the feelings, emotions and attitudes beneath them. Examine your verbal transitions. Check that they are clear, or will you add some of your own?

Indicate where you might use gestures.

When you are familiar with the material, personalise your message – make it yours:

Eliminate any expressions or words that are not you.

If you normally speak in short simple sentences, don't use long-winded ones.

Look for places where you can insert a personal example or anecdote.

Try to use personal pronouns. For example, instead of saying 'Staff will resist change on the holiday entitlement . . .' rather say 'your staff' or 'our staff', or simply just 'you' if addressing them directly. People listening to you read should feel that you are having a conversation with them.

Mark the script as discussed in the section on notes. You might also want to underline the words that carry meaning, the ones that will require emphasis.

Remember: to gain emphasis you can:

- Change your pitch, intonation and inflection

- Add force or volume
- Vary your pace
- Alter your rhythm
- Vary your attitude

Look at your audience and talk to them. Even a written speech must sound warm and caring when read. Use the word 'you'. Connect with your audience through your body language, gestures and eye contact.

Check that the language you are using is conversational in style. For example use short forms. 'It's' instead of 'It is'; 'That's' instead of 'That is'.

Hints to Help Your Reading Style

- Use fairly heavy paper
- Check the lectern is wide enough to slide the notes across easily (see note section)
- Use only one side of the page
- Use large bold font and have it enlarged
- Double or triple space
- Mark the script with all your personal instructions, pauses etc.

Easier Script Reading
Familiarise . . . . . Personalise . . . . . Emphathise . . . . . Practise

Teleprompter (Autocue)
The teleprompter, commonly referred to as an Autocue (which is a brand name) has become more popular during the last few years with business speakers. It is used by the front bench in the House of Commons, and also by TV presenters.

It consists of a one-way screen which is placed in front of you and onto which your script is projected. The advantage of this method is that the audience can see your face through the screen, and as you read the words, you appear to be looking at the audience. The whole script is prepared in advance. The speaker needs a lot of practice, ideally with video, to be able to read the script whilst looking up at the audience for quite long periods. The full script of what you are going to say reduces nerves to manageable proportions.

The text is printed on a roll of paper or computer stationery and relayed by close circuit television cameras through monitors near to the speaking point. From the monitor it's reflected on to the screen in front of you. An operator, hidden from the audience, carefully follows the speed at which you are speaking and moves on the roll of script as appropriate.

Advantages

The main advantage is that you can read the entire script and also maintain eye contact with the audience.

Print is normally large, with only a few words per line, therefore it is readily legible.

A small table top unit is available, which is suitable for boardroom meetings, and can be used by anyone who is speaking.

Hints for Use

- Preparation is the key to success. Allow yourself sufficient time for last minute changes. Send your script to the teleprompt company in plenty of time. This is particularly important if several speakers are involved. When modifications are made at the last minute, all the cues must be re-positioned.
- Always ask for a copy of the script typed on the autocue roll, so that you can practise reading aloud.
- Allow several run-throughs with the teleprompt company at the venue. It is the normal procedure for the teleprompt hire company to include some tuition in their hire charge.
- Check the height of the screen, as this can be adjusted to suit different speakers. If you place the screen vertically, this allows for a greater range of speaker's height, without adjustment.
- Consider the use of two or more screens. It gives the reader

more flexibility of movement, but remember this will need extra practice.
- Appear natural, look away from the screen now and again.
- Speak at a normal pace.
- Follow the body language advice given in chapter 9.

Rate of Speech Test
The average rate of speech is approximately 150 words per minute. Speaking rapidly makes it difficult for people to understand you, and speaking very slowly may cause them to lose patience and stop listening attentively.

To check your rate of speech, read the following article aloud and time yourself. The article contains around 300 words, and it should take two minutes to read at a rate of 150 words a minute. You may wish to use a tape recorder.

START

Speech, at the most elementary level, demands extensive mental effort. A meaning, before it takes form in a speech, is something which is not yet defined. Its communication in speech requires that it be conveyed in some kind of order. The simple fact is that we rarely achieve a continuous flow of speech. The speaker and the listener co-operate. Listeners concentrate on the message; they bridge the gaps which divide the groups of words. The speaker, on the other hand, co-operates by trying to minimise the gaps in the stream of words and make them coincide with semantic groups such as phrases.

The point to remember is that pausing is as much a part of speaking as vocal utterance. Pausing is a very basic part of speech production and has a specific function in the giving of a presentation. It permits delay – the time for thinking, for the thought process to take place. There is no need to substitute 'ah', 'er', 'um', 'well' or 'now' and the like. The listener will not find the pause unusual. Delay is simply a built-in feature of oral language. Most pauses go unnoticed because they are natural, so there is no reason to have a continuous flow of sound while speaking.

Concentrate on the idea you are dealing with, gain confidence and a sense of rapport with your audience, and your hesitations will be no longer than the minimal delays which we have come to expect, and in fact need, in spontaneous speech. Pace should not be dictated by the pressure of time on the day itself. This means constant practice before your presentation. Speak out loud in your normal voice. You can then change your script where appropriate.

END OF TEST

Now check your rate. If your rate of speech is very much slower than 120-150 words per minute, practise until you are happy with it. Also check that your script is working for you. Do you have pauses, emphasis marked? Listen to your tape recording; would that voice make you sit up and take notice?

Readability Test

Often copies of the presentation script are given to the audience after the event. Will your audience recognise it as the performance you gave? A readability test is useful to check the written materials which are distributed. The purpose is to measure how easy or difficult it is to read a piece of your writing. As a measure of readability, it is based on two factors: sentence length and word length.

1. Take a sample of your own writing, such as a letter, memo or report. The sample should be at least 200 words long.
2. Count the number of words in the passage and divide this by the number of sentences to give the average number of words per sentence. Count hyphenated words as two, and treat as words such items as numbers and symbols.
3. Count the number of long words i.e. words of three or more syllables. Disregard capitalised proper names and also words of which the third syllable is one of the grammatical suffixes: 'ed' (invited), 'es' (supposes) or 'ing' (presenting). Work out the total

number of long words as a percentage of all the words in the piece.
4. Add together the two figures i.e. average number of words per sentence and the percentage of long words, and this gives you your readability index. It is probably between 25 and 40. The lower the figure, the more easily understandable the piece is likely to be.
5. Repeat this exercise with further samples of your own writing, and take a final score.

Sentence length and word length are not the only factors affecting readability, so the index figure may be misleading. Also important are:

- Right choice of words
- Sentence structure
- Style of language (appropriate to the reader)
- Clear layout, use of headings and paragraphs
- Interesting subject
- Punctuation

Your average sentence length should be about 20 and never rise above 30 words. But if you try to write all sentences to have a length of 20 words, the result will be a very stilted style. Just write naturally with no rules in mind. If the result is rather turgid to read, then take a look at the length of the sentences to see if some need pruning.

Perhaps it is taking a liberty to classify all three-syllable words as long; for example 'area' has three syllables but only four letters; but the criterion works usefully for the purpose of this exercise. It is not that three-syllable or long words are difficult or unusual. It probably struck you that some of those you counted were straightforward, everyday terms that will puzzle nobody. The point is that a piece of writing becomes heavy to read if it contains a concentration of long words, however simple these words may be individually.

Your percentage of long words should normally be about 10 per cent or less. If it is approaching 15 per cent and there is no way of avoiding it (say, because of the technical nature of the subject) then consider using shorter sentences to compensate. Your readability index is a useful guide, but the only true test of a piece's readability is how it actually reads.

Compare your score with the following:

The Sun	26%
Daily Mirror	28%
Sunday Times Business News	30%
Daily Mail	31%
Daily Telegraph	34%
The Guardian	39%
The Independent	32%
Conditions of use on application for Access card	49%

7. How to Control Nerves

Everybody suffers from nerves. The fear of making a fool of yourself, or forgetting what you were going to say produces all kinds of symptoms.

Here are the most common:

Hand, leg, knee and whole body shake.
Palpitations and feelings of panic.
Rapid speech.
Shallow breathing.
Negative body language: predominantly, loss of eye contact, slouching, wringing hands.
Sweating, palms, underarm, whole body.
Either static or robotic body movements.
Feelings of nausea, headache, stiff neck.
Excessive 'ums' and 'ahs'.
Drying up and losing the flow of speech.

Most presenters have experienced several of the above symptoms at one time or another. There are several steps you can take to reduce this feeling of panic. Firstly, when discussing nervousness, it is useful to note the different types of fears people may have.

For example, fear of:

- The unknown
- Physical reactions to nervousness
- Losing your place
- Drying up

- Being inaudible
- People getting up and walking out
- The impression you are making on your manager, employees, colleagues
- Losing attention
- Making a fool of yourself

By acknowledging your fear, you can then examine it, and take steps to deal with it. By following the advice in *Successful Presentations* you will gain all the knowledge you need to put together and deliver a very credible presentation. This will go a long way to dispel most of the above anxieties.

Professionals will all admit to suffering from nerves. For example, Disraeli admitted that he would rather have led a cavalry charge than have faced the House of Commons for the first time, but he later became one of its favourite speakers. Mark Twain described the first time he stood up to give a lecture; he felt his mouth was filled with cotton wool and his pulse was speeding for some prize cup. Katherine Whitehorn, columnist at *The Observer*, gives this advice,

> *Even if you're quaking inside (and you probably are), come across as if you know what you are saying and are sufficiently confident to say it with some humour and not too dogmatically. The public doesn't always appreciate that the person who bangs the drum and says, 'I am right and I will brook no disagreement of any kind' is actually the person who is deeply unsure inside. The more confident you are, the more you can say, 'I think the way I would approach it is . . .' rather than 'Now listen here you must do this'.*

This is excellent advice, and links to what I said earlier, that you set the tone for the presentation. Your approach is crucial – assertive, but friendly and professional, not dogmatic.

Adopting a 'professional style' like this will give you confidence and reduce nervousness.

Jane Asher, actress and writer, has this advice.

> *Everyone gets nervous – it would be unnatural if you didn't, but remember that your audience wants to hear you. They're not against you.*
>
> *I have a little trick for calming my fright before speaking. I imagine that I've had some really terrible news, something quite devastating (in my case something to do with my family). Then I remind myself that it's not true – only pretend – or even continue my fantasy to the point where someone comes to tell me everything's all right after all. Then, having to make a speech seems so totally unimportant and trivial compared with the awful scenario I have just pictured, that I feel ashamed to be nervous and grateful that the important things in life are OK. I can swan through the speech knowing how relatively silly it all is!*

This visualisation technique is useful in helping you put the fear in perspective. By actually painting the worst picture you have acknowledged the fear, and imagined what it would be like, for example, to dry up, to lose your place. You then further develop this into a positive outcome. Now build up that picture of you giving a wonderful performance and appreciate the warm glow which this produces.

Visualisation is being used successfully in areas such as sports training, where coaches are trying to build up the confidence and performance of the athlete.

Many professional actors recommend the following method. Besides preventing fear, it reduces negative feelings like anger, anxiety, depression and fatigue; it also generates energy.

- Sit in a straight backed chair. Carry you rib cage high, but not in a ramrod-straight military position. Incline slightly forward.
- Now put your hands together just in front of your chest, your elbows akimbo, your fingertips point upwards, and push so that you feel an isometric opposing force in the heels of your palms and under your arms.
- Say 'ssss', like a hiss. As you exhale the sound, contract the muscles in the vital triangle as though you were rowing a boat

against a current, pulling the oars back. The vital triangle should feel like a tightening corset.
- Relax the muscles at the end of your exhalation, then inhale again.

Contracting those muscles prevents the production of noradrenaline and epinephrine, the fear-producing chemicals in your system. So, when you want to shake off nervousness, sit with your vital triangle contracted, your lips slightly parted and release your breath over your lower teeth on a slight hiss. You can do this anywhere.

Deep Breathing Can Also Help
Here are two exercises which are simple and can be done anywhere. I find the first particularly useful to regulate my breathing, just before I give a presentation.
One:

- Draw a deep breath into the stomach.
- Release air slowly, counting to ten out loud.
- Continue until you build up a rhythm.

Two:
This second exercise should make you relaxed and energised.

- Exhale, bending over your stomach.
- Now stand up straight and slowly breathe in deeply through your mouth.
- Repeat twice.

Be careful not to extend this for too long: too much oxygen may make you dizzy.

Don't Show Fear and Don't Talk About Your Fear

Remember that your fears are internal and the audience will not be aware of them – unless you draw attention to them. The following is a selection of some of the comments I have heard from presenters:

'I'm very nervous, it's my first time.'

'Please bear with me, I'll get the hang of it' (referring to use of the overhead projector).

'I can feel my knees knocking.'

'Look at my hands shake' (when pointing to the screen).

'I'm a bit nervous – I hope it will work' (when setting up a demonstration).

Bob Monkhouse tells the story of when he worked on the BBC 1 Talent Show, *Bob Says Opportunity Knocks*. Bob and Stewart Morris had to watch up to 70 acts a day. Morris would make notes on each relevant application form, occasionally adding a cryptic V sign. One day Bob asked, 'Is that V for victory or the symbol for sticking up two fingers?' 'That my dear man,' explained Stewart, 'is a reminder that the performer in question is a vibrator. Take the last singer. Good voice and unaffected by the tremors in her knees. But to conceal the shakes she had today, I'd have to get a cameraman with a bad hangover to tremble in tempo.'

Bob then assumed that they wouldn't use her, but Stewart explained that no performer ever quivered through an entire show. The shaky period passes. Therefore it would mean a few extra rehearsals, and some reassuring words. If she still shook, then no hand-mike.

So before moving on to what you can do about nerves, keep in mind that:

- Fear is a normal experience. The fact that you are afraid indicates that you are like other people.
- Fears are not well founded: speakers do not die while speaking or even faint. Audiences usually receive them sympathetically.
- If you are well prepared you almost always give creditable performances.
- Nervousness tends to disappear with added experience.

- Presenters seldom look as frightened as they feel. Audiences rarely see a speaker's knees tremble or a flushed face.
- The tension you feel at the beginning of your presentation is helpful.

Presenters who no longer find an audience stimulating are likely to be dull. Use the nervous energy to sharpen your delivery and concentrate on getting your points across.

Some Ideas to Help
Often presenters are nervous when they first stand up to speak. This is natural and providing you have done all your preparation the nervousness will disappear once you get going. If it continues after this initial period one of the reasons can be that you are concentrating on yourself and not on your audience. The following is a checklist and some advice on how to control, or at least to conceal your nerves from the audience.

- Prepare thoroughly – 90% preparation, 10% perspiration.
- Visualise yourself doing a great job.
- Rehearse thoroughly.
- Build in audience participation – takes the heat off you.
- Adopt a pleasant attitude – your audience are willing you to succeed.
- Use positive language.
- Be enthusiastic and friendly – it will rub off on the audience.
- If you feel that your throat may dry up, have some water near to hand. (Always move water jugs off the front table to the side before you begin. I have witnessed a presenter's overheads rendered unusable because he failed to do this.)
- Always stand to give a presentation; it adds to your credibility. If you are conscious of leg and hand shake, a full lectern might help. This is useful when speaking to a large group. The audience won't be able to see your legs, and you can hold the lectern on either side. (Relax your arms, do not grip tightly.)

- Keep hands out of your pockets and find something purposeful to occupy your hands.
- Avoid alcohol, coffee and other stimulants if possible. If you must, have enough only to relax you.
- Make sure that you are standing in a comfortable position with the equipment you will be using to hand. If you don't feel comfortable with your surroundings, it will show.
- Try some of the suggested deep breathing exercises given earlier. Aim to be a professional.

Finally, some degree of nervous tension must remain with a good speaker always. You must learn to harness the asset. To aim to be without it would mean that you had killed a priceless quality. Some years ago Sir Ralph Richardson said, 'What makes a professional is that you are used to being afraid. You accept fear.'

8. *Delivery*

DEVELOPING GOOD SPEAKING HABITS

The ability to project a professional business image depends on a person's ability to speak effectively, i.e. to speak in such a manner as to achieve clear, unambiguous, relaxed and thoughtful verbal communication.

Inevitably, in a book on successful presentations there is much emphasis on developing skills to control not only what you say, but also how you say it.

What you say will be determined by your preparation, your audience and your objectives.

How you say it depends on your personal habits of verbalisation, including emotional attitude, accent, speech patterns, volume, tone, pitch, pacing and projection.

Delivery

Many people worry deeply about how they speak and how they sound, and this anxiety often prevents them from expressing themselves as fully as they would wish. We spend 80 per cent of our time speaking and listening, and yet these are often the areas which are neglected. Unfortunately, lack of these two skills may detract from an otherwise professional presentation.

We often judge people by the way they talk. A study conducted by Albert Mehabrian found that almost 40 per cent of the total image that you project during the first few minutes of meeting someone relates to how you put your message across. This obviously has an important lesson for a presenter who wishes to project a good first impression.

Dr. Lillian Glass, an American communications specialist, conducted research to determine how people really feel about common talking habits. People in the survey were asked about eleven frequently encountered talking habits: Did they find the habits annoying, and, if so, how much? Here are the results. The numbers are percentages of those polled.

Survey Results:

	Annoys a lot	Annoys a little	Total Annoyed	Does not Annoy	Don't Know
Interrupting while others are talking	59	29	88	11	1
Swearing or curse words	56	28	84	15	1
Mumbling or talking too softly	37	43	80	20	0
Talking too loudly	32	41	73	26	1
Monotonous, boring voice	27	46	73	26	1
Using filler words such as 'and um' 'like um' and 'you know'	33	36	69	29	2
A nasal whine	34	33	67	29	4
Talking too fast	24	42	66	34	0
Using poor grammar or mispronouncing words	27	36	63	36	1

Delivery

A high pitched voice	24	37	61	37	2
A foreign accent or regional dialect		5	19	24	75	1

In the business situation, your audience will be judging you partly by how you talk. They are making decisions about you, which may or may not be accurate, and they will act on these perceptions. As a professional you want your vocal impression to supplement your other abilities. The first step to improvement is to look at and listen to yourself. Objectively, see and hear yourself the way others perceive you. A video-camera and recorder are excellent tools to help you assess your performance, and also to monitor improvements. A tape recorder is needed to help you analyse your voice.

If you don't have a video recorder, then stand in front of a mirror and use a tape recorder.

Most people are surprised, and often horrified, when they hear themselves for the first time. Their voice does not sound in the least as they had imagined. It seems to sound higher in pitch and thinner in quality. Often there are mannerisms which are totally unexpected – you speak slower or faster than you think, you sound affected, or sloppy with unfinished consonants, or your accent may be heavier than you thought. Worst of all, you may sound plain, flat and boring. However hearing yourself on tape does not necessarily give a whole impression of your voice. The machine is more sensitive to some frequencies than to others. For example I have found that a woman's voice usually comes out higher than it actually is. However there are many other impressions, such as communication through the eyes, face and body – all of which influence how we hear a person and tell us something. It is interesting what images we create of people on the radio, based purely on voice. It is often a shock, pleasant or unpleasant, to see the actual person – the voice and body may seem mismatched.

I know an excellent speaker, a sales director, who tapes all his speeches, his sales pitches, everything he needs to know. When he is travelling he pops his cassette into the car sound system and listens to himself talk. By doing this he hears his strengths and weaknesses. Any new ideas or additions are spoken into a little hand recorder which sits on his passenger seat. These are later added to his script. I can certainly recommend this method, as I have used it myself in the past. One particular occasion was when I was asked to speak at a Burns supper: I recorded my speech on tape and played it in the car on my way to and from work. This helped me rehearse the words, in particular the flow, and also the links between ideas. One of the possible disadvantages of doing it this way is that it can sound stilted, but obviously this is the first stage of your rehearsal when you are concentrating initially more on what you say rather than how. The how will come later when you have analysed your script and have the structure, the flow and the links perfected.

If you are rehearsing at home, look in the mirror to see how you are making the sounds. Observe your body language i.e. your facial expressions and stance. The video recorder is particularly useful as you can observe all the aspects of verbal and non-verbal communication. At this stage you are primarily concerned with your voice. Body language is covered in detail in Chapter 9, but it is worth jotting down any observations at this stage, e.g. posture, facial expression, gesture.

Here is a communication test which includes some yes-or-no questions. By answering them, you can learn what it is about your speech that you don't like.

Stand in front of the camera and talk to yourself for about a minute or stand in front of a mirror and tape-record yourself. Some suggestions on what to talk about are:

- What is the best/worst presentation which you have attended either as a presenter or as a member of the audience? What made it memorable?
- Your personal goals.
- Your objectives for reading this book.

Stand up straight, pay attention to your posture. Hold your head erect and look beyond the camera as if talking to your audience.

Look at yourself and make mental observations as you talk.

The Communication Test

A) Voice
Does your voice sound:

Yes No
☐ ☐ Shrill or squeaky

☐ ☐ Too loud

☐ ☐ Too high

☐ ☐ Monotonous

B) Pronunciation
Do you:

Yes No
☐ ☐ Mumble

☐ ☐ Mispronounce words

☐ ☐ Have an accent or dialect

☐ ☐ Mispronounce vowels

C) General communication skills
Do you:

Yes No
☐ ☐ Talk too fast

☐ ☐ Talk too slowly

☐ ☐ Tail off at the end of sentences

☐ ☐ Use clichés, slang, jargon

☐ ☐ Say 'um' or 'okay' or use fillers a lot

Other comments:
e.g. body language

Now turn off the video or tape recorder and rewind it. Imagine that you are criticising someone other than yourself. Prepare to view and listen to everything objectively. This is a good exercise to do on your own, but is even more valuable if you can persuade a friend or colleague to give you feedback.

These questions will help you become more aware of exactly what you do or don't like about the way you sound: your vocal quality, pitch and pronunciation. You can now set about improving your vocal image.

Your voice is part of your personality, a statement of yourself. It is worth remembering that no voice is wrong if it is communicated adequately. On one of my courses, a participant expressed concern that one of his colleagues had commented on his accent, saying that it was hard to understand. When he came to do his presentation, I and the other 12 members of the group gave him feedback on his voice using the feedback sheet. Apart from his fast rate of speech at the start (caused mainly by nerves) and his virtual absence of pauses, the clarity was good, and with further practice he was able to pace himself better and therefore communicate more clearly. Learning to do this gave him more confidence as he now felt more in control.

Here are some of the most important areas to consider when assessing your verbal communications.

Clear Diction

This is without doubt the most important element in clear verbal communication. Many people in business tend to speak carelessly, slurring their speech without precision. Naturally you are influenced by the particular regional accent of your birth, your parents and the general community. Everyone has an accent, and if you can put your message across so that you are understood by those who are listening to you, then your accent is an asset, and can only count in your favour. If, however, you have a strong regional accent, together with careless speech, then get help to improve it, or it will become a liability. Remember that we said earlier that your audience formulate first impressions about you based on how you sound. A poor opening may influence them to switch off for the remainder of your communication.

Modulation

The enemy of modulation is monotony – speaking in a one-note drone. Most people are not guilty of monotony, but are guilty of dull and lifeless speaking. Modulation of the voice depends on momentary change of pace, of pitch and of power; and on pausing. Grasp this comforting point from the beginning, that mastery of these attributes not only allows you to appear more accomplished to the audience, but also allows you to speak more easily. To speak monotonously, or just without colour or tone, is not disagreeable to those listening but more fatiguing for you, because you are using only one set of muscles.

Projection

People normally lack resonance of voice because they do not make full use of the lungs and the many resonant cavities of the head and upper body; because the jaw muscles have become rigid, the mouth has become tight and the tongue physically lazy.

Humming is the key exercise. Hum on the letter 'M', which means that the lips to all intents and purposes are closed and you are using the post-nasal cavities. The word to have burnt into your brain all the time you are humming is 'forward!' Speaking from the front of the mouth is essential for good audibility; for the ability to carry your words to the furthest that your eyes must look; for an insurance against dropping the voice or biting off the ends of the words, and for sheer selfish ease of speaking. Strive to throw the sound forward so as to use the hard palate, which is a sounding board for the voice. The proof that you are humming correctly is that very soon the inside of your lips, particularly of the upper lip, becomes warm. Probably it will tingle, rather like the outside of your lips used to when, as a child, you played on a comb covered in tissue paper, but not so pronounced. The tingling and the warmth, in that order, should be felt within a minute. Quality of humming is more important than volume.

When you have mastered this simple technique, then you can hum in odd moments. You can hum when you are strolling in the garden or stretching your limbs in the office; when you are walking through the noise of crowded streets or in the peace of a London square. You can also hum when driving or held up in your car. (Make allowances in this case for the fact that your posture will not be good.)

Go into a quiet room, stand with 'relaxed authority' and close your eyes so that you can concentrate on the sound. Hum in your normal pitch as quietly as you can, concentrate on holding the pitch and bringing the sound forward. Then, being most careful not to change the pitch, gradually increase the power. This mastered, increase and decrease the power whilst still holding the constant pitch; this exercise is also excellent for enlarging the capacity to breathe. Repeat the exercise, still with the greatest care, first on a lower then on a higher note. Help yourself to succeed by visualising the stream of air ascending from the bottom of your lungs to the lips. Then occasionally let the lips very slightly open and close to test that they are held firmly but not tightly. This will produce a 'M-M-M-M' sound. Later on, lessen the monotony by humming some music of a marked rhythm, always with a deliberate beat, never with the casualness normally associated with everyday humming.

Many presenters do not throw the voice forward and several speak right at the back of the throat; hence the special importance of this exercise. At first do it for three or four minutes at a time; and when it is mastered strive to keep up the custom for a couple of minutes daily. Relax as you practise it.

These exercises will help you develop the foundations for a good presentation voice – authoritative and friendly.

If your throat is husky or your voice tired, gargle with a

teaspoonful of salt, the right measure of glycerine of thymol or similar products in half a tumbler of warm water. If in trouble sometime before the meeting, frequent gargling can strengthen the voice.

Finally, I must mention the value of reading aloud. Why not choose some of your favourite poetry? This can give you knowledge of, and so potential command of, language at its best. A further benefit is that this may inspire you with great and beautiful thoughts which can remain with you for ever.

It is best always to start speaking quietly. Stand up or sit down, as you please. Speak a line or a thought, if need be, over and over again. Chisel your speaking – by pause, by change of pace, of pitch or of power – until you are satisfied with the result. Always speak to bring out the meaning, and not just individual words. When you are happy with your progress, imagine that you have an audience. Notice how the eyes and features, and occasionally the hand join in: how the body is gently alive in the effort – and how this combined effort makes speaking so much easier. Try this poem, a particular favourite of mine, by William Blake:

The Tiger

> Tiger, Tiger, burning bright
> In the forests of the night,
> What immortal hand or eye
> Could frame thy fearful symmetry?
>
> In what distant deeps or skies
> Burnt the fire of thine eyes?
> On what wings dare he aspire?
> What the hand dare seize the fire?
>
> And what shoulder and what art,
> Could twist the sinews of they heart?
> And, when thy heart began to beat,
> What dread hand, and what dread feet?

> What the hammer? What the chain?
> In what furnace was thy brain?
> What the anvil? What dread grasp
> Dare its deadly terrors clasp?
>
> When the stars threw down their spears,
> And watered heaven with their tears,
> Did He smile His work to see?
> Did He who made the lamb make thee?
>
> Tiger, Tiger, burning bright
> In the forest of the night,
> What immortal hand or eye,
> Dare frame thy fearful symmetry?

Remember that the voice may vary with your mood or your physical condition. If you have a really important presentation to make, strive, if possible, to relax for thirty minutes; lie down, or at least put your feet up. Build this in as part of your preparation.

Slurring

This is the running together of words or parts of words. Speakers who do not normally slur their speech sometimes do so in public through nervous desire to get it over and done with. This need not worry the beginner, so long as he is aware of the fault. It will cease as his confidence grows. It is habitual slurring of speech that is really dangerous. It is not uncommon to hear an exasperated adult tell a child to 'open your mouth when you speak, I can't hear a word you say'. A lazy tongue causes most of this trouble; when this is allied to smothered production due to a partly closed throat, the result is a mumble.

Exercises for the Tongue

If you say the sentence 'What have you got in the bed?' you will see the importance of an active tongue, because it could so easily have been rendered: 'Wa' 'an you go' in the bed?'

A) Say 'Lah-lah-lah-lah-lah' like this, rapidly, in sets of five.
B) Repeat using 'Lah-rah' in sets of five.
C) Imitate a telephone bell – bree-bree! trilling the 'R' thoroughly.
D) Memorise and practise the following:

> In Tooting, two tutors astute,
> Tried to toot to a Duke on a flute;
> But duets so gruelling
> End only in duelling
> When tutors astute toot the flute!

Pitch

Excessively high pitch is most commonly found in women. The voice always sharpens when fear, anxiety or anger are felt. The cure is a) to be aware of the condition and b) to practise relaxation exercises whenever you have a moment in private to do so.

Nasal Speech

Usually due to laziness of the soft palate and, in part, to uneven control of breath. The simplest exercise is to open the mouth wide and say rapidly: 'Ah-ng', 'ah-ng', 'ah-ng' as often as you can manage comfortably on one breath. Now vary it by saying 'oy-ng', 'oy-ng', 'oy-ng'; next, alternate the two; 'ah-ng-oy-ng' etc. This invigorates the soft palate, stopping the sagging which leads to nasality. This is best practised in private.

Unconscious 'Er's' and 'Ah's'

These are the little bleating noises we make when we are searching for a word. It is an unconscious habit, and many people are unaware of doing it.

This habit can be eliminated by thinking out the sentence first and then speaking it, rather than beginning with half an idea and having an 'er' in the middle while you think of the rest.

It is important to eradicate this habit because not only does it distract your audience to the point of irritation, but it breaks up the rhythm of your speech.

Rate of Delivery

Rate is the speed at which a person speaks. In everyday conversation people usually vary their rate to fit what they are saying. But some people are stuck in a rate rut. They always speak either very fast or very slowly. Extreme rates of speech in presentation are distracting to listeners. They will defend themselves by mentally tuning you out. Varying rate to suit your words keeps listeners interested. It also signals listeners as to what is important.

Here are some practical tips on how to vary your rate appropriately. First, remember that listeners must process new and/or complex ideas as words come out of your mouth. Thus, use a standard rate that is somewhat slower than the everyday conversational rate. A slower rate helps listeners hear and interpret what you are saying. Vary your rate from this standard depending on the difficulty or importance of what is being expressed. Slowing down provides thinking and response time, while speeding up prevents much consideration. Here are some circumstances in which a change from the standard rate is a good idea.

Slow your rate when:

- The words are difficult or express a complex idea
- You are reading a quotation or generalisation
- The words deserve special attention

Speed up your rate when:

- You are reading a list to make a point, but you do not want people to remember individual items
- You want to produce a comic effect

Diction

Try the following extract to practise your articulation. Repeat it at speed without scamping a syllable.

The major-general's song from *The Pirates of Penzance*

I've information vegetable, animal or mineral,
I know the Kings of England and I quote the fights historical,
From Marathon to Waterloo in order categorical.
I'm very well acquainted too, with matters mathematical,
I understand equations, both simple and quadratical,
About binomial theorem I'm teeming with a lot of news –
With many cheerful thoughts about the square on the hypotenuse.

Finally, here is a simple exercise you can follow to help you create a better sounding image.

Relaxation Exercises

1. Head rolls: Slowly rotate the head to the right, back around to the left, and forward. Do this five times, beginning at the right, and reverse five times, beginning at the left.
2. Shoulder rolls: rotate your right shoulder forward and leave it there for three seconds. Rotate your left shoulder forward, leaving it there for three seconds so that both your shoulders are forward. Next rotate your right shoulder back and then your left shoulder back so that both shoulders are back. Repeat this exercise ten times.
3. Facial relaxation: Close your eyes. Then consciously relax your forehead, eyebrows, eyes, cheeks, nose, lips, jaws, ears and neck, concentrating on each facial part for approximately five seconds. For the next twenty seconds visualise a relaxing fantasy.
4. Relaxation breathing (see chapter on nerves)
5. Consonant exercises: Say each one of the following sounds as fast as you can for as long as you can on a single breath.

   P F TH T S K H

6. Vowel exercises: Say the following vowels in progression, dropping your jaw further for each vowel sound. Be sure to exaggerate the vowel sound and the opening of the jaw.

EE IH EH AH
AW UH O OO

Communication Checklist – Your Voice
Effective communication is an important skill in business life. There are some pitfalls, but there are also many devices you can use to give you clear and effective communication.

- Use the outward breath and relax
- Start positively and loudly
- Let the pitch of your voice flow up and down the scale from high to low and back again, just as the pitch of a little child does when speaking
- Use emphasis, pauses, inflections. Vary the pitch and volume. This will give light and shade to what you have to say
- Use a warm and resonant voice. Avoid sounding harsh, too weak, too loud or flat. A monotonous voice is very wearing to listen to
- Build your point vocally. Add emphasis and drama through the way you actually say your words by stressing the most important words and phrases. Light the important ones and shade the less important ones
- Avoid 'oh' 'uh' and 'um' and phrases such as 'OK' and 'you know'. Most presenters have the occasional one in their speech, but if you overdo this, the audience will begin to expect them and start counting
- Make sufficient use of the pause
- Make sure that your voice rises when you ask questions and falls when you make statements
- Clearly articulate each sentence, phrase, word and syllable. Give full value to all the sounds in your speech
- Display a lively amount of vocal energy. By making the words sound interesting your audience are more likely to be enthusiastic listeners
- Make sure your thoughts forge ahead helping to build your argument

Delivery

- Have enough breath to finish each sentence on a strong note. Often 'ums', and 'ahs' are a result of insufficient breath. The 'um' is inserted to fill the void before finishing the sentence or phrase
- Use the rhetorical question to involve the audience; it also gives variety to your speech patterns
- Vary your pitch, force, volume, rate and rhythm. Catch people's attention by getting noticeably louder at important points. Listen to politicians giving speeches. The best political speeches are those which use the devices listed here, when there is no ambiguity as to which of their issues they see as 'key'
- Check your speed (use the test provided). The average presentation speech rate will fall approximately between 120-150 words per minute. John F. Kennedy was reputed to average over 300 words per minute in his speeches. If you listen to any of them, notice how quickly he skims over the unimportant words, but makes great use of the pause and emphasis when he reaches his salient points – then rushes on again. What happens is that the unimportant words are used like a string, to link up the key information, but the key information is remembered.
- Do not drop consonants (e.g. tryin', plannin')
- Use correct pronunciation

Observing good presenters, you will almost certainly see that they are committed to their words. They show enthusiasm for what they say and how they say it.

Use of the Microphone

Unless you must, do not use the microphone. At the beginning of this century, members of parliament, quite unaided, had to address audiences of more than 5,000 at election time, Today, the microphone is a regular fixture in many function and conference facilities. One of the disadvantages is that it encourages the speaker not to use the full range of his voice, and the microphone is often totally unsuitable to high echoing ceilings (an example of this is the use of the microphone in churches).

The use of a microphone cannot improve the personality of a speaker; it can cause loss of personality. On some occasions however, it may be an advantage.

Advantages of Using a Microphone
Presenting to Large Audiences

- The microphone is an excellent aid when presenting to very large audiences e.g. conferences, particularly when wired to amplifying speakers around the hall. It ensures that everybody in the audience can hear.

Answering Questions

- It is useful when you have to answer questions. This is the technique used by Rosabeth Moss Kanter, mentioned earlier. It also means that if the situation is appropriate, you could sit, and adopt a crisp conversational tone.

Content

- It is likely that if you use the microphone you will cover more ground, as you speak faster than when you use the voice alone.

Overflow Meetings

- Occasionally, the microphone is used where there is an overflow meeting, when many of the audience will be able to hear the speaker but not see him. In this case it would be a courtesy to both the speaker and the audience, if the speaker walks through the 'unsighted' rooms, and is perhaps introduced informally. It can also work for close circuit television. This helps build a bridge between speaker and audience and smoothes the way for the message to follow.

Open Air

- The microphone is without rival in the open air. It is often seen in conjunction with the above, at large events, from the Pope speaking to tens of thousands in St. Peter's Square, to memorial services and media sporting events.

Control

- At public meetings the microphone can help the chairman take and keep control if the situation is disruptive, and things are getting out of hand. The chairman has every right to gain control. I have seen this done very effectively at political meetings to deal with hecklers.

Conversation

- If a speaker wishes to speak in a relaxed, conversational manner to a large audience, he can remain seated for his speech and have the microphone placed about one foot away from him.

Disadvantages

Used correctly (and rehearsed) there are few disadvantages to using the microphone. Remember that it is another technical detail which you have to check as part of your preparation. As a speaker you will encounter various types:

a) Fixed on a stand which can be adjusted to the speaker's height.
b) Fixed on a short stand or rest to place on a table.
c) Attached to a lectern. It is often a good idea to have a microphone at each side of the lectern.
d) Attached to a jacket or dress with a small clip – or hung around the neck. Advantageous if you wish to walk about. Because the microphone moves with you, you can do this without your voice fading. Be careful with this type of mike that you don't get tangled in the wire.
e) Hung from the ceiling. Height adjustable. The disadvantage is that they are static – usually set where the speaker will stand.

Often microphones will be a combination of the above. Increasingly popular with professional presenters is the cordless mike. This has many advantages, but one small disadvantage is that part of the apparatus has to be carried on you, so strong pockets are advisable.

Microphone Technique
As a presenter you will almost certainly use a microphone at some time in your career. Here are some hints for its use:

Whatever mike you choose, always practise with it first. The technique of using the microphone depends mainly on two considerations – the proper tone of voice and the proper distance.

As to tone, increase your power rather than heighten your pitch. As a rough guide, imagine you are throwing your voice. Make use of control. When you begin speaking, watch the reaction of those sitting at the back of the room. Is their body language telling you it's too loud? I saw a humorous example of this at a large presentation recently, when the audience put their hands over their ears when the presenter introduced himself. Alternatively, are their faces strained?

Rehearsing beforehand will solve these problems. This is particularly important if you are one of several speakers. The previous speaker may have adjusted the microphone to match his or her height, and that could leave you bending or stretching – either way it does not look professional, nor comfortable. As to height, any position from just below the chin to the level of the chest should be suitable. The angle of the microphone, straight or tilted, and the relation of your position to the audience will decide your exact choice.

If you wish to make an emphatic point, take a careful step back (almost rock back). This is a technique to avoid 'feedback'.

Once you begin to speak, don't touch the microphone. If it squeals you may have accidently touched it; take your hand away and it should stop.

If you hear a loud popping sound from the mike, try adjusting it so that you are speaking into it at an angle instead of straight on.

If several speakers are to appear on a panel to answer questions, a microphone each is advisable if the occasion is to flow smoothly. If only one mike is passed between them, continuity is lost.

Always check that there is someone around with knowledge of the sound system. Don't rely on the confident assurances of 'it'll be all right on the night'.

Be aware of unguarded words in front of a live microphone; a mutter to the chairperson that 'they were a dull lot' as you sit down, may stifle your applause if the words boom out over the public address.

Switch off noisy equipment, such as air conditioning fans or telephones, which may be a distraction.

Don't fondle the microphone lead whilst you are talking.

Avoid wearing nylon shirts and blouses. The instrument may crackle if it rests on a shirt front made of nylon.

If it sounds wrong, then stop and have it adjusted before you continue. Stay calm, raise your voice and say for example, 'Will someone kindly switch on this wonderful piece of equipment?' With perseverance the engineer should hurry over to sort it out. If it still plays up, then you will have to make the decision as to whether your voice will carry without the mike.

Check with your audience. Say, 'Can you hear me at the back?' If not, perhaps take a few steps forward, or adjusting the position of the mike.

Experience will show you how to make best use of the microphone. Have the confidence to fall back on your own voice power if you need to.

9. Body Language

Before you have opened your mouth to speak, your body language has been sending signals to your audience, about how you feel. If the message conveyed is nervous, non-assertive and vulnerable, then everything that follows is transmitted in that frequency, and constantly fails to make an impact.

You should consciously use body language when you are presenting.

Use it to:

- Invite a response or a contribution.
- Develop empathy and build trusting relationships.
- Present yourself effectively – develop your image and self-confidence, beat the stereotype. Remember, first impressions last.
- Give feedback (e.g. I am listening, interested, concerned, enthusiastic).
- Set the scene so as to relax the recipient (e.g. at a selection interview) or to alert them to your feelings (e.g. when about to give praise, criticism).

When considering body language, always stay within the limits where you and the recipient feel comfortable. Uncalled for displays of body language create unnecessary risk.

Research conducted by Albert Mehrabian shows that the sum of the message you communicate is made up as follows:

>　55 per cent appearance and body language
>　38 per cent how you sound

7 per cent what you say

A combination of all three elements creates a very powerful message, and the signals received by the audience will say 'This presenter is – confident – competent – in control.'

The personal body language or non-verbal element of your communication must be positive to make a good impression. The components of the message you send can be divided into these three groups:

Voice
pace of speech
clarity
pitch
volume
tone
expressiveness

Your Body
appearance
facial expression
eye contact
posture
the way you move
the gestures you make

Relationship to Others
use of touch
sensitivity to and use of personal space

You must use body language consciously and deliberately. Research has shown that when the verbal and non-verbal messages are in conflict, the audience will believe the non-verbal message. An actor manages to produce laughter when he combines one non-verbal gesture with a verbal statement to the opposite effect. The disparity between verbal and non-verbal is always enough to make the audience laugh. I have seen this work very successfully, when a managing director of a large company presented his annual report to senior staff.

> *Sales have increased by 25 per cent . . . the reasons . . . (he went on to list these) . . . firstly, our superb sales team . . . (up went a slide of a very dishevelled and disreputable looking team) . . . secondly, our new customer service centre . . . (slide of an old tumbledown building) . . . and so on.*

His staff loved this approach. The message was good news, made more interesting by the injection of humour. This is an alternative approach to use if the topic which you are presenting could become tedious, e.g. lots of statistical data. The verbal/non-verbal approach is particularly useful when you are giving good news to your audience, or the subject lends itself to the humorous approach.

One consultant on non-verbal communication states that: 'If a man tells you he has an open mind on the subject, and at the same time he clasps his hand, you can be confident that his mind is already made up.'

Of all body language, it is bearing that communicates presence the most quickly and effectively. Bad posture, sloppy sitting, slumped standing, weary walking, are the common faults.

The message you send out is always interpreted as 'Who cares?'

Remember you want to send out the confident, competent, and in control message.

Here is some advice to help you do this:

Posture
The key to holding yourself well is the simple but contrasting phrase 'relaxed authority'. A batsman or a golfer, before he shapes to hit the ball, stands with relaxed alertness. When I am putting the finishing touches to an oil painting, I stand upright yet relaxed to ensure the steadiness of hand.

Stand easy and upright, the stomach in, the chest well held, the head well poised and the feet comfortably apart. Keep the feet still.

Then, as you speak, turn smoothly from left to right, using all the joints given you for this purpose – the ankles, the knees, the hips and the shoulders. Particularly give the head the fuller mobility it commands through the top two bones of the vertebral column, allowing it to move sideways, upwards, downwards, forwards and backwards. This is a natural action, and will help you as a speaker as it gives the nervous tension and nervous energy a healthy outlet. Tension that might have been shown in fidgeting, excessive feet movements or gesturing, is used up unnoticeably.

Learn to stand tall with your head and chin up, your rib cage high, your stomach tucked in. When you are standing, push your head up as high as you can – feel it stretching. Then let your shoulders slump, as if you were trying to lift a heavy object from the floor.

Keep your feet slightly apart with the weight evenly distributed. If you hold the legs close together, your movement is distinctly cramped. By all means, occasionally shift your ground – say, every five minutes – but do so unhurriedly. There must never be any unnecessary movement of any part of the body. Check that all your movements are purposeful.

Several circumstances may justify movement:

- If you are demonstrating something, you may need to move closer to your listeners so they can see better
- If you want to write on the flipchart, or change an overhead slide
- If you move forward into the audience to take questions
- If you want to reinforce a change of mood. For example the speaker might stand behind a table or lectern for the first part of the presentation. For the second, he may move forward to take questions or give a demonstration

I know a marketing manager who practises his posture by standing on a hard chair, and speaking to an imaginary audience.

If you speak sitting down – by custom of the meeting, through injury or illness, when answering questions after a speech – move from the hips. This position of relaxed authority is not only for appearance but, as always, for good breathing and the comfort of your throat.

Be aware of your posture when listening creatively. Sitting back in a passive position makes you look slumped and inert. By projecting your upper body towards the speaker, you are thrusting yourself actively into the scene where the action is. Slumping whilst standing or sitting is tiring. A good posture keeps down fatigue and exhaustion.

Try not to turn your back on the audience. To help you remember this, think of the words 'Full Frontal'. (This may remind you to smile now and again.)

Gesture

A relaxed, responsive and smooth series of movements helps the audience to relax. It will also be easier for you to listen creatively, to smile and gesture as appropriate. Erratic movements signal bad news to the audience: the message is that you are tense, nervous and worried. Such an attitude in turn evokes a negative response: uncertainty and distrust. There are two ways most people move about i.e. smoothly and slowly, or jerkily and swiftly. Aim for the former.

Gestures can be tremendously powerful. Avoid unnecessary gestures. An unnecessary gesture is one that does not aid you in communicating your message. Examples include habits such as pen or pencil fondling, hair curling, beard stroking, hand in pocket change rattling.

Gestures should always be natural, expressive and clear. The key to gesturing is spontaneity and moderation. Always make gestures outwards, from the centre of the body. Harold Macmillan, when Prime Minister, acknowledging an audience as he arrived at a large meeting would swing both arms above his head like a boxer before a fight – but he would never dream of doing so during a speech. A videotape recorder is useful to record your performance. You will then be able to decide if your gestures are appropriate for the occasion, and check that they correspond with your words. Never use a half gesture, it shows lack of confidence. If, for example, you are using a pointer to emphasise a point on your overhead slide, extend the arm fully and with confidence.

To sum up, gestures should be natural and also linked to your personal style and the size of the audience. Generally the larger the audience, the larger the gesture.

One sure way of including gesture successfully in your presentation is to generate enthusiasm for your subject. Enthusiasm rubs off on your audience. Think of speakers who are 'fired up' about their subject. They will gesture naturally. Another benefit of generating enthusiasm is that the voice will appear naturally interesting. It is rare to hear an enthusiast talk in a monotone.

Facial Expression

The face is the most expressive part of the body for revealing attitudes and feelings. This is important to realise because people tend to focus on a speaker's face as they listen. They use what they perceive there to help them make judgements about the speaker. Does he 'look' sincere? cynical? friendly?

Eye Contact

Eye contact is probably the main expectation listeners have of facial behaviour. Eye contact should be a simple, natural expression of your interest in the audience. It allows you also to monitor their level of interest and understanding, as well as helping to establish rapport and gain attention. In certain light conditions, the pupils will dilate or contract as a person's attitude and mood changes from positive to negative and vice versa. When someone becomes excited, their pupils dilate to up to four times their normal size. Conversely, an angry or negative mood can contract them to what are often described as 'beady little eyes'.

Remember that in presentations, the audience is made up of individuals. Make contact with each of those individuals, but not in a pattern.

When you enter a room, particularly just before your presentation, look around and make contact with as many people as possible.

When you make eye contact with someone, you are making a commitment. It is this commitment that helps develop and maintain trust and rapport with the group.

Always look at the questioner when answering questions, but don't forget the rest of the audience. A rough guide to eye contact in this situation is 80 per cent to the questioner and 20 per cent to the remainder of the audience. Try not to favour some members of the audience over others. It is very important to give lots of eye contact to those who are interested in what you have to say (or to the chairman or the decision maker).

Mrs Yve Newbold, company secretary of Hanson plc., is very experienced in giving presentations and speeches. Here is what she has to say about eye contact: 'I try to look at the audience in a sweep that is like my Flymo doing the lawn, a sort of left to right and back again arc, starting at the front and working down the audience.'

Most people have a bias toward one side of the room. Generally there are two reasons for this:

1) When speaking from the centre of the stage, the presenter often focuses on a friendly face at one particular side of the room, and gives them good eye contact.
2) When speaking off-side (often in conjunction with a flipchart), the side of the room diagonally opposite the flipchart position gets more attention.

To avoid this, when you get up to speak direct your feet to the centre of the room, full frontal to your audience, feet firmly on the floor and slightly apart. (See equipment section – use of flipchart p. 134)

Expression
Unless the message is meant to be serious, look pleasant; smile when you can. Cultivate a pleasant and positive expression. But keep it in check. Smile at individuals when you answer a question, or make reference to them.

It's a psychological fact that facial expressions alter emotions and that in time we grow in tune with our most usual expression. So if you confront your audience with a face like a wet weekend, sooner or later that's how you're going to feel.

Friendliness begets friendliness. It does not mean a permanent veneer of smiling without meaning; it must be natural. A twinkle in the eye automatically causes a twinkle in the voice. This quality is of vital importance in all speeches, particularly in the after-dinner type. According to Professor Paul Ekman, there are three types of smile.

- The Felt Smile

This is the natural smile, a genuine expression of a positive emotion, which usually lasts between two and four seconds. It's unique in that it uses the orbicularis oculi muscle around the eye, as well as the zygotic major muscle (the muscle which turns the corners of the mouth upwards). In other words, when someone is smiling because she means it, you can see it in her eyes.

- The False Smile

As used by failed Wimbledon tennis players. It tends to be more lopsided than the real variety, and to last a second or two longer. And it never reaches the eyes.

- The Miserable Smile

Usually used when someone is trying to put a brave face on. This is the most lopsided of them all.

But a smile doesn't have to be genuine to make you feel better. In an American study, a group of actors were asked to play out various expressions while their heart rate, blood pressure and skin temperature were monitored. In every case, these functions all calmed down when the actors were smiling, and doctors believe that smiling produces hormones which have a positive influence on body functions. Looking happy can actually pick you up!

Think of this just before you stand up to speak, smile and tell yourself that you are going to enjoy making this presentation. Imagine the applause you will receive afterwards.

Hands

One of the most common questions I am asked on presentation courses is 'What do I do with my hands?'

People do many things with their hands, most of them unnecessary and distracting to an audience. Here are some of the most common faults.

- Clutching the back of a chair
- Grasping table or lectern
- Playing with hair, jewellery, face, notes, pointers
- Fiddling with loose change or keys in pockets
- Wringing, rubbing
- Posing:-

– the fig leaf position; hands clasped in front of the body
– the housewife; tidies up paper, notes in front of him/her
– the Duke of Edinburgh; hands clasped behind back
– the frusted orchestra conductor; waves pen, pointer in the air.

Most presenters have a favourite pose, such as hands loosely held in front. The secret is to find a position which suits your style and comfort level. Never clasp your hands together, or hold a wrist, tightly. Artificial control reveals tension – and can actually stiffen the expression. Whatever position you adopt, don't let your hands flit about, clasped for a few seconds, then on the table or into the pockets. Properly used, movement of the hands is part of your expression of thought. Here are some ideas of what you might do with them:

- Cradle them just under the ribs – the right hand gently resting on the left palm with left thumb locking both together.
- Clasped in front of the body

- Held by the side at arm's length, the backs showing slightly (this suits a quiet speaker or a quiet passage in a speech)
- Holding cards to nestle in the palm of the hand (lift forward and up when referring to them)

Many presenters like to hold cards in the palm of their hand, a pen if writing on the flipchart, or a pointer if using overheads. There is no hard and fast rule on this, except that whatever you decide, make sure that it is not the centre of attention. The audience are there to listen to you, not to see you shuffling your note cards, snapping the top of your pen, or pulling the pointer in and out. I have seen a presenter hold all three items at the same time. To make matters worse, for convenience, he left off the top of his red marker pen. Some time into his presentation, and much to the amusement of his audience, he stuck the pen into his mouth with unhappy results. I have also witnessed on several occasions the marker pen top fly into the corner of the room. Try to hold only one item in your hand, preferably your cards; any more, and you create distraction.

Personal Space
Psychologists have established a few basic rules of distances between people.

Here is a rough guide as to how close people should and should not be for normal business situations.

1. Lecture Distance

When you are more than 12 feet from another person, you are said to be at 'lecture distance' from him or her. This means that there is a minimum of intimacy between you and your companion. It requires a raised voice to communicate adequately.

2. Business Distance

The second range of distance between people varies from 12 to four feet. If that range of distance separates you and your listeners, you are considered to be at a business distance.

3. Personal Distance

The third range of distance between people measures from four feet to one and a half feet. At this range, you are at what psychologists call a 'personal' range. This particular distance is usually reserved for business associates who know each other fairly well, or who are working together on a project, or who are discussing something that sometimes rises above the strictly routine office situation.

4. Intimate Distance

The fourth range of distance between people is at one and half feet or less. This range is reserved for business friends, such as a long-time partner or board room colleagues or acquaintances with whom you have been on a business basis for a long time; for most private business confidences, and for members of the opposite sex in whom you are seriously interested.

Your presentations should be conducted at 'business distance'. When you come forward to take questions, keep your distance from the questioner, otherwise he may feel intimidated. People feel threatened when their personal space is invaded. Fill the gap between you with positive body language i.e. warm friendly style, good eye contact.

Positive Attitude
This is one of the key elements to successful presentation. On the surface attitude is the way you communicate your mood to others. When you are optimistic and anticipate successful encounters, you transmit a positive attitude – people usually respond favourably. When you expect the worst, this mood transmits itself to other people, and they tend to avoid you.

Attitude is a mind-set. It is the way you look at things mentally –

whether you see situations as either opportunities or failures, whether you view giving presentations as a chore or an opportunity.

Quite often, your feelings about tackling a subject stem from memories of past experiences. If these experiences were not positive then anxiety can set in. Sometimes it is necessary to pre-programme our feelings; many sports coaches train their athletes this way. Part of the method is to use visualisation technique. For the presenter, this can be used as part of the final preparation.

The steps are:

1. Put your presentation together using the checklists and advice in this book.
2. Rehearse thoroughly
3. Before your actual presentation:

- Do some relaxation exercises (see chapter 7 on dealing with nerves)
- Make yourself comfortable, and close your eyes
- Picture the room where you will do your presentation. See the audience and notice how friendly they seem. See yourself stepping up front to speak. You have prepared thoroughly and are looking forward to having a friendly conversation with them. Feel yourself doing a terrific job as you 'think' through your presentation.
- Hear their applause when you end.

If I have an important presentation to make, I usually go through this sequence the evening before (usually when lying in bed thinking of the next day). Many people find it useful to use visualisation technique in the period just before they stand up to speak.

Maxwell Maltz, who advises salespeople in selling skills, also stresses the importance of developing a positive attitude. He talks about self fulfilling prophecy i.e. if you think positively – you are likely to get positive results. Negative thoughts produce negative results. You, as the presenter, need to develop this positive attitude.

Often, it is not easy to do, but the fact is that a positive, friendly attitude on your part will build bridges with your audience. You will also feel less nervous and more confident.

Here are some hints:

Always use positive language. Eliminate the negative. Here are a couple of phrases heard from presenters: 'You will probably find this topic boring' (manager talking about new administrative procedures). 'I'll read out these statistics, as you probably won't be able to see them' (accountant explaining department expenditure).

Never use the word 'boring' or any other negative. If the topic is boring, why are you talking about it? If you use words like 'boring' the audience will switch off, and in fact become resentful that you are taking up their time.

If you have prepared a slide that the audience can't read, why should they waste time looking at it?

Avoid words such as 'hopefully', 'I'll try to . . .' – for example 'hopefully, at the end of the presentation . . .' Instead say 'at the end of the presentation.' It sounds more confident and assertive. (This approach also makes your audience feel more confident in your ability.)

If you deliver your presentation in an enthusiastic manner, you will reap many benefits.

1. Your audience will warm to you, and therefore they will be more attentive. (Audiences generally adopt the tone of the presenter i.e. enthusiastic presenter = enthusiastic audience; dull, boring presenter = audience switch off.)
2. Enthusiasm will help.

a. Your voice will sound more interesting: an enthusiastic voice breathes life, not monotony.
b. Your body language will be more positive i.e. verbals and non-verbals will match. Natural expressions, gestures, posture will result.
c. Enthusiasm is catching – enthuse your audience.

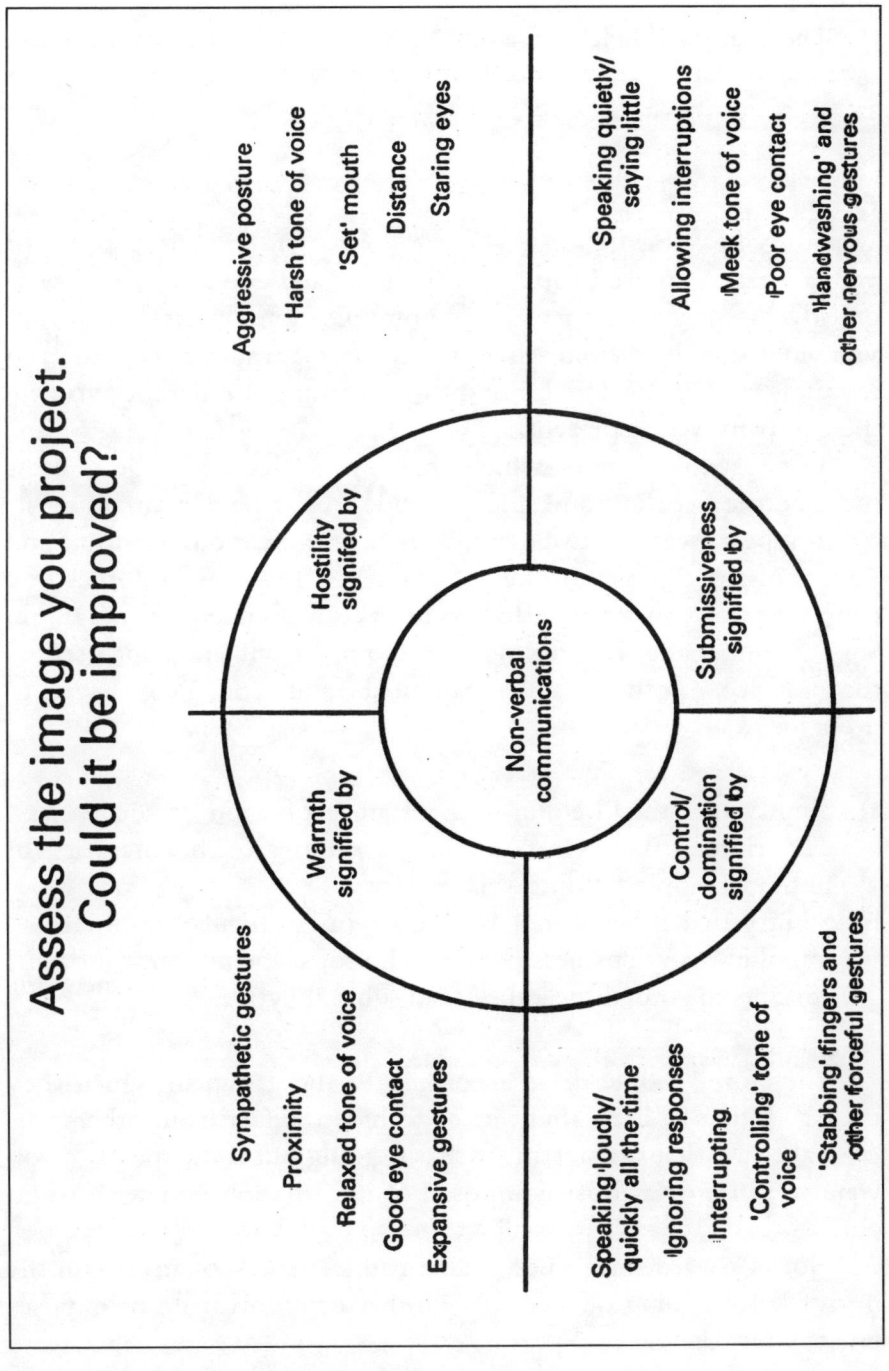

The chart will help you assess your non-verbal communication.

First Impressions Last

Dress

When giving presentations, you are your own best visual aid – or your worst. You are in full view of your audience, who will very quickly assess your non-verbal communication. Everything about you sends signals: the old school tie, the Armani suit, a woman's too revealing neckline, scuffed shoes, bad grooming. Remember **you** are the company you represent.

The essential factors which shape your decisions about dress must be the occasion and your attitude to the people attending it. Your appearance should be appropriate to you, your position and your message. People dislike the phoney, so whatever clothes you choose to wear, make sure that you feel comfortable in them. If you are uncomfortable, this feeling of discomfort will transmit itself to the audience. Clothes make a statement about you. People tend to dress to:

a) Signify that they belong to a certain profession or social class. The clothes they wear are like a uniform. The majority of business people fall into this category.
b) Signify that they do not belong to any particular group. Also found in many business people, who for some reason want to be considered something other than what they are.

Therefore, people dress according to the group in which they belong. Either to brag about it, or to hide the fact from others.

Take care that the statement that is going out is the message you want to send, or at least composed of information you wish to go out.

Noel Coward once said: 'I take ruthless stock of myself in the mirror before going out. A polo jumper or unfortunate tie exposes one to great danger'.

Here is a checklist of some things to avoid:

For men:

- Ill-fitting suit
- Bulging pockets (avoid coins, handkerchiefs, keys)
- Pens/pencils in top pocket
- Excessive aftershave
- Unbuttoned shirts
- Loud ties
- White socks
- Light coloured shoes
- Flashy cuff-links, tie pins, jewellery
- Ostentatious belt buckles
- Short socks
- Check zips and buttons are secured

For women:

- Bare legs
- High heels, short skirts, low cut blouses
- Distracting jewellery, jangling bracelets, earrings
- Large belt buckles
- Shoes with scuffed heels
- Lumps and lines – check what is underneath
- Standing against bright light if wearing lightweight clothing
- Excessive make up, perfume
- Distracting hairstyle, e.g. hanging over face
- Taking your handbag to the lectern/table – leave it to one side
- Check zips and buttons are secured

General hints for both men and women:

- A dark business suit, teamed with a smart shirt or blouse, is seen as 'professional' for both men and women.
- Take care with shoes. Scuffed heels are very noticeable on

women; carry a spare pair of shoes in the car for driving. Shoes are particularly visible if you are presenting on a raised platform.
- If you have to travel to the venue, then carry your outfit in a suit carrier and change when you arrive.
- Adapt your dress to the people you are addressing; you don't want to dress exactly like them, but choose a style similar to theirs. When in doubt, dress on the formal side, but try to add some flair; audiences don't want to look at deliberately drab speakers.
- Don't wear clothes that need to be adjusted when you stand up or sit down.
- If you wear glasses, remember that heavy rims will hide your face and interfere with eye contact. Stay away from strong tinting or light sensitive lenses that darken under lighting. Many professional speakers avoid these problems by opting for contact lenses.
- Use your glasses to effect by taking them off once or twice during your presentation. Use them to give your gestures added impact. Take them off at the end of your presentation to take questions.
- Aim to be well groomed and well turned out – fresh and neat, then forget your appearance, let your personality shine through.

Develop Your Own Style

The famous philosopher and mathematician, Blaise Pascale, noted: 'When we see a natural style, we are always astonished and delighted'.

True style comes from within, and a person with style is said to possess 'charisma'. Style and commercial success are synonymous. The presenter with style is as brief as impact and message permit. There is no single successful style in business presentation, but presenters who seek success will project their personal individuality: body language is part of your style. If you discover that your natural style is to talk very quickly and move in jerky spasms, try to slow down the rate of speech, and examine your body movements. The likelihood is that if you can control your speed, the movements will also slow down and become less jerky. Keep your own 'natural' style. If you are comfortable being voluble and moving your hands and body as you speak, only tone this down if it is excessive and causes a distraction. Don't try to change the total you, but make small changes for improvement.

I have watched presenters who have broken all the so-called rules of body-language, loud excessive body movements, infringements of body space, who have performed with excellence – their natural style of humour, friendliness and enthusiasm have turned a negative to positive. Conversely I have seen presenters try to 'adopt a style' that quite clearly is far removed from their own natural style. The result is a wooden and lacklustre performance, punctuated with incongruent body language.

Feedback is an essential ingredient of good communication. Just as your audience will be reading your signals, you will be reading theirs!

What to look for:

Think of your audience like flowers: closed, and they are defensive, negative: open, and they are warm, receptive.

Head down = negative. Head comes up = interested. Head to the side, perhaps with finger vertical up to the cheekbone = evaluating, deeply interested.

If you are boring, covering known ground, then the audience gets impatient, tapping, twitching, and fiddling with things. If they have had enough, they turn to something else, such as diary or another paper. They look at their watch or the clock; they even look longingly at the door!

If they are bored they become lethargic, stop looking at you and put their heads down on their hands, eyes half shut. People move all the time. Look for feedback, and match how you perform to how they react. Unless you must stick to a script, be driven by the audience, not your notes. If the audience turns off, you waste your time and theirs.

Appearance and Body Language Checklist

- Dress smartly and be well groomed. Remember 'PMA' – your

dress should be appropriate to your position, your message and your audience. It should reflect your personal style.
- 'Upright' posture (i.e. head up, shoulders back, chest out, stomach in, back straight).
- Stand up – full frontal to your audience.
- Get as close to the audience as possible without invading their personal space.
- Smile occasionally – but not at individuals, unless specifically referring to them.
- Project your voice to the back of the room.
- Make gestures and movement appropriate to your individual style, but always purposeful.
- Speak with enthusiasm – bring some passion to your subject.
- Personalise your language – pretend you are speaking to a friend.
- Use comfortable language that 'fits' your style.
- Use 'you'. Many presenters are victims of the 'we' or 'I' syndromes. Involve your audience by using the word 'you' as often as possible.
- Relax and enjoy yourself.

Summary

Appearance and body language are important elements to consider if you wish to create a positive and professional image. Examine your body language and work to improve your unique personal style.

Finally some advice to speakers from Peter Ustinov, a man with his own unique style.

> *The main thing is to have a point of view, and to release your imagination in the parkland of your subject, like a dog. Then as the dog does, rely on instinct. Don't go on too long. If the public is wonderful, stop a little short of total triumph. If they find you boring, go on a little longer than necessary, just to punish them. Also resist the temptation to laugh at your jokes before reaching the point. The audience may find this inhibiting, to the point of not wishing to join in the laughter, your laughter. There are many rules, but as usual, they are only to be broken.*

10. Visual Aids

Advantages of Using Overhead Slides
One of the most popular visual aids is overhead slides, or OHPS. In addition to being quick and inexpensive to make, overheads provide:

- Illumination

The large projection area, usually 10 × 10 feet, permits a lot of light to reach the screen. As a result you can use it with a fairly large number of people. Overheads can also be used in a fully lighted room.

- Speaker Control

Not only can the group see the slides, but so can you. This offers you better control of the group and more eye contact. You will be able to be more attentive to their reactions.

- Speaker Identification

Overhead slides are the part of your presentation that illustrates what you are saying. You also have the flexibility to manipulate your slides; you can turn the projector off entirely to make a verbal point, can reveal material on the slide a little at a time, or can point to specific words.

- Facilitation

Overhead projectors are easy to use. The new models are quiet enough to offer little distraction.

Videos and Films

Videos and films are being used increasingly by the larger companies. These media are not only hard to update inexpensively, but also can't be controlled by the presenter. Most videos are designed for continuous viewing. Their advantage lies in their power and sophistication. They are particularly useful for putting across strong messages. They are often used to 'kick-off' sales presentations. The material shown lays the foundation for the presentation to follow. Used in this way, the audience all start from the same knowledge base. Videos and films also provide a pleasant change of pace for lengthier presentations.

35mm Slides

These are less flexible than overhead slides. Their main advantage is that they can effectively dramatise a difficult concept. Their chief disadvantage is that they turn the audience's attention away from you, and also require a darkened room to be viewed effectively.

Your voice has to be especially lively and interesting if your presentation takes place in darkness, particularly if the slides are shown after a meal. Despite their obvious disadvantages, in many cases slides can be invaluable for larger audiences. Some situations really call for their use: for example to present in an instant what would take many words to convey. Slides also give the speaker flexibility; individual slides can be replaced or updated fairly easily without changing the whole set.

To produce effective slides:

- Build your slides around what you want your audience to remember (your objectives)
- Establish good rapport with your audience before you begin the slide show.

To establish this link with your audience, you could give:

With room lights on:

a) **Introduction**
- A face to face short introduction to your presentation (tell them what you'll tell them)

Main lights off: (if possible leave some lighting on – it is a good idea to arrange for a spotlight to shine on you during the showing. This means that the audience can see you and you can also read your notes).

. . . then link into . . .

b) **The body**
- (tell them – with slides)
  . . . link into your reprise . . .
- (tell them what you've told them)
  lights up . . .

c) **Close** – face to face with audience

If you use this sequence, you begin and end your presentation with audience eye contact. The slides are used to present the body of information.

- Don't leave a slide on the screen longer than you have to. When you have finished talking about it, go on to the next one.
- Prepare the technical aspects well. Check that:
  the projector is in good condition
  the projector is in focus
  the slides are placed in the carousel the right way round. To do this:

- hold up the slide to the projector light so that you can read it.
- place the slide in the carousel upside down, so that the top of the slide enters first
- number each slide
- check the slides are in order and practise with the remote control

- Use only as many slides as you really need. Don't waste the audience's attention with superfluous information.

If something goes wrong with the slides – if you drop the carousel, or they are out of order, or the light fails, or there is some other emergency – take a break and try to fix it.

The presenter is the best person to operate the projector, by using the remote push-button control. If someone else is operating it, then rehearse together – you must have confidence in the projectionist. Work out any codes to exchange information. Cueing can best be done by marking the script with cue keywords.

Flipcharts

Flipcharts are excellent aids, particularly useful for group discussion and brainstorming activities. They are best used with small groups of up to about thirty people. There are several types on the market, including one which consists of laminated boards (available in different colour combinations). It is used the same way as the standard flipchart, but is re-usable. One of the main presentation faults with this piece of equipment is that the presenter sometimes obscures the chart.

Where to stand to avoid this:

Stand to one side of the chart stand – on the right if you are right-handed and on the left if you are left-handed. To check correct positioning, try this: Grasp the edge of the chart with your left hand and move it slightly back to your right. Your arm should not be fully extended. Think of your gripping arm as a hinge. This means that you will cover part of the board as you write. By swinging back on the 'hinge' you can reveal what you have written to the people on your right.

Here are some other hints for using the flipchart:

- Write in large clear lettering
- Use capital letters
- Don't talk and write at the same time

- Use key words instead of sentences – this cuts down on writing time.
- If ink goes through the paper, use every other sheet. This is often a good idea anyhow, as you may want to go back and add some information. It's also easier to flip over two pages at a time.
- If you are speaking in a long narrow room, put the flipchart on a raised platform. This will help people at the back of the room see what you've written at the bottom of the page. (If there is no platform, then write only on the top two-thirds of the page.)
- Don't close yourself off from your audience by pointing to the chart across your body. If you are right-handed place the chart to your right.

Many presenters do not like using the flipchart because they fear that their writing is illegible or that they can't draw diagrams or straight lines. Practice will allay these fears. There are many special types of charts on the market, which will help solve the problem – lined or graph paper, also a vast choice of templates to help draw accurate shapes.

Use the pencil technique: Take a pencil and prepare your flipchart sheets in advance. Lightly sketch out your graph or diagram in pencil. At the appropriate time in your presentation, you then go over it in pen. I have seen this work very successfully in a technical presentation. The presenter built up his diagram on the flipchart to help explain a particular aspect of a computer system. (This technique works equally well on the whiteboard.) You can use it to help with spacing and to indicate starting points for headings, and it can be used to present statistical data. Key words can also be written on the side of the chart. The audience can't see the pencil marks, and they act as an *aide memoire* for you.

When preparing the flipcharts in advance, label each page. Place a tab of white sticky tape folded neatly at the left hand edge of the sheet and label. Do this on each page. Labelling helps you readily identify pages as you progress through your presentation, and also makes it easy for you to locate pages should you want to refer back to them.

Models and Objects

Models and objects are limited to small groups. Models need ongoing input from the presenter to come to life. As with videos, models work best when the situation really calls for them.

When you pass out objects, samples, or other materials as visual aids, you will lose a certain amount of attention from the group. Use the time when they are being passed round to summarise or to describe the object. Don't try to introduce new points at this time.

Whiteboard

This visual aid comes in many forms, from the large screen size to the flipchart size. The larger boards are particularly useful for presentations which require a big display area, for example technical presentations, where diagrams and flow charts can be built up and left on the board for reference. If you decide to use the whiteboard, remember that you must use the appropriate type of dry marker pen. If you use ordinary chart pens on the whiteboard, you will find it difficult to remove the writing. Invest in some of the special cleaning solution made for this purpose. A special penholder attached to the board could help prevent mixing up the different types of pens.

Note: If you find yourself with a board displaying the previous presenter's artwork (written with the wrong type of pens) and you have no cleaning solution, try this: write over the original artwork with the correct whiteboard dry marker pen. You will find this will rub off easily with a duster.

Whiteboards have been around for some time. Many variations are now available, for example the copy board. This allows you to write on a dry wipe surface, and then copy the result down to A4 size for handouts. The electronic whiteboard is a touch-sensitive whiteboard that captures a written message or drawing and transmits it down a telephone line to a compatible monitor, projector or printer. A smaller version of this is also available. Using the same technology, the sender uses a desktop writing/sketching tablet, either A4 or A5 size. An optional disk storage unit allows received images to be recalled at will for later study and evaluation.

There is an apparatus on the market which offers a combination of boards – flipchart, magnetic and whiteboard all in one.

Magnetic Board
This is useful to secure charts, maps etc., using magnetic strips or shaped magnets. You can see the possibilities of building up, with cardboard cut-outs, jigsaw fashion, the plan of, say, a new office layout. Magnetic string can be used to link one part of a flow chart to another. Titles, arrows, labels can be added using the magnets.

Flannel Board
This is the first cousin of the magnetic board. It is a rigid board, usually covered in flannel or felt, which works on the same principle as the magnetic board. Instead of magnets, special sticky tape is used. This type of board is generally used at exhibitions to display company information.

Chalkboards
Chalkboards can also be used as visual aids for small audiences, if you follow these hints:

- Use damp not dry dusters.
- If not wall mounted, check stand, legs, pins are stable before using.
- Use a pointer to emphasise particular areas.
- Use only key words, not sentences. This will avoid having to turn your back on the audience for long periods while you write.
- Clear the board when you have finished talking about what's on it.
- Use yellow chalk. It shows up better than white.

Display Board
This can be used for an informal discussion and can be placed on a desk or table top. You know exactly what each chart shows; you have identification on the back of the chart which follows. So you can stand behind the charts or on one side facing your listeners,

turning each page as you proceed. It is particularly useful for intimate presentations, and is easily portable. Its main advantage is that you can give your listeners good eye contact. It is also available in a variety of sizes, one of which folds down to a briefcase. The graphics displayed should be of high quality, no less than if you were presenting the information to a large group.

Props

These are another way of enhancing your presentation. When used correctly they can put you more at ease, help make your presentation clearer and more vivid, and enable you to seize and hold attention.

The most significant guideline for using equipment or props is that you should practise using them beforehand. It is embarrassing when you expect a machine to do one thing and it does another – or nothing at all!

- Pick up your prop only when you are ready to use it
- Hold it high enough for everyone to see it
- Hold it so it does not hide your face
- Talk to the audience, not to the exhibit
- Put it aside when you have finished with it

The more visual aids you use, the more practice you will need. This is particularly the case with many of the computer-based systems.

Handouts

There are three major uses of handouts in a presentation:

1. To reinforce important information
2. To summarise action items for the audience to follow up
3. To supply supporting information that you don't want cluttering your visual aids

Consider handouts as part of your preparation stage. Work out how many you will need, and also when you will give them out.

VISUAL AIDS

This will vary depending on the type of presentation. A general rule is that if it is not necessary for the audience to refer to the information during your talk, leave them till later. However, at large customer presentations, sales brochures and publicity materials are often available before the presentation begins. This method can elicit interest and help stimulate activity at question time.

Always tell your audience that you have handouts for them at the beginning of the presentation. If you don't, someone is sure to ask. Also, it is frustrating for the audience to jot down copious notes as you speak, only to be told at the end that the key information is covered in the handout.

You may want to give out copies of your overheads as handouts. The key rule for handouts: They must have a clear purpose and contribute something you could not convey verbally.

Say it with Pictures
The best visual aids are a kind of shorthand. Charts and illustrations are the visual aids used most commonly and effectively by the creators of slides, transparencies and charts.

Charts
Whether a diagram, map or original artwork, illustrations make visual aids visual and keep them from looking like duplicates of your speech. Charts are flexible and can show graphs (bar, pie, or line), cause and effect, and organisational relationship. Consider using cartoon type visuals. I have seen these used successfully in pharmaceutical and medical presentations.

Flowcharts
These can be used to show stages of development, or a number of steps in a sequence.

Pie Charts
Use pie charts to show parts of a whole at any one point in time. Pie charts are designed to show total amounts and also their parts, calculated in percentage or fractional segments; for example when

illustrating expenditure in the different company areas such as marketing, sales and advertising.

There is an excellent video on slide presentation made by Video Arts. It outlines all the do's and don'ts. In one particular scene John Cleese plays the manager who is giving his colleague advice on slide presentation.

Picture the scene . . . The audience is assembled and the presenter puts up a pie chart, saying 'and now you can see at a glance how your money has been spent'. Camera pans to audience whose necks almost turn through 90 degrees as they try to decipher the information. Giving feedback later, Cleese advises the presenter: 'The only person who benefited from that slide was the osteopath – my neck still gives me gyp when I think of it!'

The moral is to make sure that the headings on the pie chart can be read easily without the audience having to turn their heads.

Line Graphs
Use the line graph to illustrate variations over a period of time or to show relative facts; for example, if you wish to compare production figures between 1988 and 1992 for production outputs which vary over this period of time.

Bar Graphs
Comparative information can be shown in vertical or horizontal bars, the length of the bar representing the value. Bar graphs are flexible and easy to read.

Organisational Charts
These charts depict the flow and functional relationships of a business or group. The structure of the organisation will be immediately obvious: departments, titles, responsibilities. In today's fast growing, fast changing organisations, you may often need to show and update this information. For this reason presenters put updated organisation charts through the photocopier to make an overhead slide. This seldom works. Almost certainly the printed chart will

prove unsuitable to reproduce on an overhead. The lettering is usually too small. Better to give this as a handout.

Using a Pointer

Pointers should be used to make a quick visual reference on a pictorial chart or to trace the relationship of dates on a graph.

Hints:

- When using a pointer, extend the arm nearest the information you are emphasising
- Don't make a half gesture – extend your arm fully
- Keep your shoulders facing the audience
- Don't play with the pointer (no frustrated orchestra conductors please)
- Retract the pointer and put it down when not using it

Headings

For a professional finish to your visuals, give them a title. Choose the typeface which best suits your need.

Subject Title

This type of title is used when it is not necessary to convey a specific message but only to provide information, as in the example below:

SALES FIGURES

Thematic Title

Used to tell the audience what information they should get from the data provided, for example:

SALES IN 1991 WERE UP 20% OVER 1990

Assertive Title

Used when you want to give the audience your opinion about what conclusion they should draw from the information given. It is often used in persuasive presentations, for example:

WE SHOULD FOCUS OUR SALES EFFORT ON THE SOUTH-EAST

Storing and Cataloguing Transparencies

When the presentation is over, you will want to store your visuals for reference and future use.

Transparencies can be stored in clear pockets and placed in a ring binder. A sticky label attached to the front of the pocket should state the subject and number reference.

If you have used cardboard 3M frames then label with subject and number on the frame. Store in the frame boxes, or in a record carrying case bought for a few pounds from W.H. Smith. These cases come in different colours, are easily portable and hold a fair number of overheads. I use different coloured boxes for different types of presentations.

It is worthwhile taking the time to store visuals carefully. They are then easily located when needed.

Lastly, practise good slide management. Find a method that you are comfortable with. For example, placing slides in a binder on the left of the projector, and as you show each one, place to the right.

In summary, visual aids can enhance your presentation, when used and chosen with care. Remember that you, the presenter, are the main visual aid, and if need be, you should be able to carry off the presentation without them. The following checklist will help you choose the appropriate visual aid for the occasion, and also ensure excellence in their use.

Video Checklist

1. Do my visual aids enhance my presentation?
2. Are my visual aids
   Clear?
   Simple?
   Bold?
   Varied?
3. Are they visible to all members of the audience?

4. Are they numbered?
5. Are they in order?
6. Have I completed my 'what if' list?
7. Do I have spare felt markers, flip charts?
8. Do I have a contingency plan?
9. Have I clear lines between visuals?
10. If I am showing slides in a darkened room, have I considered how I will read my notes?
11. If I am using handouts, have I counted and checked them fully, and decided when to distribute them?
12. Have I noted on my cards when to turn on and off?
13. Have I varied the way I will present the information?

Visual Aids

Advantages	Disadvantages
Overhead Projectors • Ideal for showing pre-prepared statistics or diagrams • Can be used to reach larger audiences • Transparencies can be economically produced • Can be used in a variety of ways, e.g. can be built up, overlaid, revealed step by step. • Can be used in normal room light	• Distracting – often fan cooled which gives off background noise. • Speaker must be careful not to obscure the screen • Projector can block view • Can suffer bulb failure

35mm Slides • Bright sharp image • Easily stored, carried • Suitable for formal/large audience presentations, professional photographic artwork	• Needs darkened room • Presenter loses eye contact with the audience • Difficult for audience to take notes • Artwork can be expensive • Needs lots of rehearsal – particularly if assistant is working projection
Flipcharts • Flexible and easy to use • Readily available, cheap and easy to pre-prepare • Can use pencil technique • Information can be build up, referred back to. • Easily portable	• Suitable only for small audiences (less than 30/35) • Can be difficult to write on quickly
Whiteboards • Similar advantages to blackboards • Cleaner to use • Usually provides large writing surface	• Limited to smaller groups • Generally not portable – found in training/board rooms • Need special dry marker pens
Blackboards • No parts to go wrong • Flexible • Mistakes easily corrected • Roller boards provide large writing surface	• Chalk – messy to use • Creates a 'back to school' atmosphere • Suitable for small groups only
Physical Objects/Models/Props • Need little description • Audience can see and touch the actual object • Often easily available	• Can be time consuming handing around objects • Only suitable for smaller audiences

11. Question Time

When to Start Thinking About Questions
Think about questions during your preparation period. When you have put your presentation notes together, read through them and try to anticipate the sort of questions you may be asked. Put yourself in the audience's shoes – if you were sitting in the audience, what sort of questions would you ask? Also think about possible objections. If you do this at the preparation stage, it will give you an opportunity at least roughly to outline possible answers. If your colleagues have spoken on a similar topic or to a similar audience, ask for their help. They will be able to advise on the type of question or objection that may turn up. You won't be able to anticipate all questions, but just thinking about them at this stage may make you less nervous about taking questions on the day, and you will be more effective in handling the unexpected. Another advantage in rehearsing questions and answers is that they often highlight weaknesses in your argument. Ambiguity can also be exposed.

Rehearsing for the Q & A Session
It is important that you rehearse with someone who can give you objective feedback. Often when you are very knowledgeable and closely involved with a subject, it's possible to arrive at a point where you are talking in your own jargon, and not fully explaining the logic of your arguments. If your subject is highly specialised, try to find someone with a similar degree of understanding of the subject with whom you can rehearse. During your rehearsal period, analyse the questions being asked, and the reasons why they have been posed.

Is the question:

- Relevant/Irrelevant?
- Referring to material which should have been included in your talk?
- One which is sure to be asked?
- One which will be covered later in your talk?

Look at these questions and try and analyse why they have been asked. Is it because of lack of clarity, illogical argument, information overload, missing material? They may be questions which can be answered in handout material. I once attended a presentation where the presenter, a manager in the health service, was extolling its virtues. At question time he was asked if he himself practised what he preached. With some embarrassment he admitted that he contributed to private health care. He then spent five minutes blustering, trying to justify his actions. He will clearly prepare this question when he repeats this presentation.

Prepare your answers carefully, including additional research into related data not included in your presentation. You will feel more confident if you take this supplementary material along with you on the day. Then if, for example, you are asked the price of a product, or a supplier contact (or whatever is relevant to your topic) during question time you can look up the information during coffee break or lunch.

Keep in mind that you won't be able to give all of the answers all of the time, but your audience will appreciate you getting back to them with the information they require.

When to Allow Questions – Set the Ground Rules
Firstly, always inform your audience in your introductory remarks when you will take questions.

For example: 'If you have any questions, please stop me at any time, and I will be happy to answer them' *or* 'At the end of my talk, there will be a question and answer session. I would appreciate if you could keep your questions until then.'

It is common in a small group situation to allow questions throughout the presentation. In this case questions are easier to control, and time constraints may be less pressing. In general, it is easier for the presenter to take questions at the end of the presentation. However, if the subject is technical or of a complex nature, then plan to take questions during the talk. Often this type of presentation requires understanding of specific concepts before the listener can proceed to the next level of understanding. If you allow questions during the presentation you need to plan how you will do this. For example you may decide to break up your presentation into three or four sections. To help you keep in control, questions could be invited at the end of each section.

Questions during presentation	Questions following presentation
Advantages • Allows the audience to understand each piece of information before going on	• Presenter has more control over his time and material
Disadvantages • Need to control your time effectively • You may run out of time • The answer may be contained later in your presentation	• Unless you build in audience interaction, the audience switch off before question time

Questions To A Panel

In this case it is advisable to allow questions immediately after each speaker has finished. Often if the audience have to wait until all the speakers have spoken, the last few speakers tend to get most of the questions. Questions taken after each speaker in this case serve to help 'break up' and also add a 'change of pace' to the proceedings.

This has happened to me at a conference where not a single question was directed at me. I had spoken early in the morning, and panel questions were scheduled for late afternoon. If you are involved as an organiser in this type of panel discussion:

- Arrange that each speaker answers questions after they talk. Set a limit, say a maximum of ten minutes. Your audience and presenter will appreciate this opportunity, and won't feel disappointed if they're not asked questions later.
- At the conference where I spoke, there were eight speakers, four in the morning and four in the afternoon, followed by panel questions. If it's not possible to have questions after each speaker, then arrange to divide up the day, for example:

a.m.   Four speakers – followed by questions to them

LUNCH

p.m.   Final four speakers – followed by questions to them
        Panel – any other questions

Panel questions are valuable provided each speaker has also had an opportunity to answer questions earlier.

ARE THERE ANY QUESTIONS?

Four simple words that can make or break a presentation.

Questions invite participation. They prove that the presenter is aware of the audience, and that he is willing to elaborate on his topic. Yet the question and answer session is an area of presentation which fills many presenters with fear. The main fears centre around the feeling of being out of control, and a feeling of vulnerability (you can be asked anything, and even worse – you may not know the answer). Fortunately, these fears vanish if you think of the question and answer session as something you can control.

To keep control:

- Set the ground rules for questions

- Limit the kind of questions: 'I will be dealing with questions related to the subject I have covered.'
- Keep control by moving closer to the audience
- Remain standing, give good eye contact
- Show confidence by laying down your notes and giving the audience your full attention
- If you are taking questions at the end, reserve the last few moments for yourself: 'I'd be happy to answer any questions, but I would like to hold the last few minutes for a summary.' If you do this you can recover from a particularly awkward last question by leaving the audience with your positive note.

You may be surprised to know that presenters look more natural when answering questions, mainly because defences are down and they are not thinking about how they look, or sound, but are concentrating on their audience.

Listen to Your Audience
Dr. Albert Einstein, in giving his formula for success:

$$X + Y + Z = SUCCESS$$

said that X represented hard work, Y represented play, and Z represented ... 'The ability to keep your mouth shut and listen'. Listening – in your case to questions and comments from your audience – means more than hearing or appearing attentive. It means being actively absorbed in what is being said, gaining clear insight into what is meant and what is implied and into why it was expressed in one way rather than another. Skilled listening on your part will help others to be objective and keep the discussion on target. It is also essential in encouraging participation.

As well as being the speaker, there are times in the presentation where you will take on the role of listener. Listening skills can be divided into two categories: passive (silent, yet attentive) and active. Often we fail to pick up the messages on the emotional line, or we may pick them up, but pretend not to and ignore them. We may be so emotionally involved that we fail to hear what is said. If the gap between words and emotions (head and heart) is small, the message will be received. If, however, the gap is large, the listener will be confused.

The major processes of active listening fall into four areas:

1. Interpreting

Sometimes it is appropriate to interpret what the speaker is saying. However, be careful of negative reaction from the speaker who may feel that you are deliberately distorting the intended message for undeclared reasons of your own. Giving attention to your questioners helps them off-load negative feelings and experiences which get in the way of clear thinking and effective action. Active listening should not be seen as a mere technique for influence. It is only useful in influencing if the listener is genuinely attentive and values the other individual's point of view. At times, silent listening is the most appropriate response. Most question times will present opportunities for both passive and active listening.

2. Observing

Careful, non-evaluative attention and eye contact while listening, automatically aids the speaker to express what he wishes to say. This provides a warm, accepting atmosphere for the speaker's thoughts, ideas, attitudes and values. Observation tunes the listener in to the speaker's words and the emotional 'music' which accompanies them, often revealed by facial expressions and body language.

3. Reflecting Data

This process, often referred to as 'paraphrasing' is akin to holding a mirror in front of the speaker, reflecting back phrases as you hear them. This increases clarity and lets the speaker know that you are hearing accurately.

4. Reflecting Feeling

As you become familiar with the speaker's emotions and the 'music' behind the words, reflecting them back will test your perceptions, as well as giving information and feedback to the speaker about his feelings. This is particularly useful if words and emotions seem incongruous. Reflecting feelings provides continual testing and expressing of understanding.

Listen carefully to what is actually said, right to the end. There is always the danger of listening only at the start, and thus failing to grasp what is really being asked. This applies particularly if we are anxious about possible hostile questions: it is easy to assume a questioner is being critical when he is actually being supportive.

There are many barriers to good listening habits. Here are some of the most common:

1) *On-off Listening*
This unfortunate habit in listening arises from the fact that most of us think about four times as fast as the average person speaks. Thus the listener has three-quarters of a minute of spare thinking time for each listening minute. Sometimes we use this extra time to think of our own personal affairs, concerns, or interests and troubles instead of listening.

2) *Open Ears – Closed Mind Listening*
Sometimes we decide rather quickly that either the subject or the speaker is boring and what is said makes no sense. Often we jump to the conclusion that we can predict what he or she knows or will say and there is no reason to listen, because we will hear nothing new if we do.

3) *Subject Centred Instead of Speaker Centred*
Often we concentrate on the problem and not the person. Detail and fact about an incident become more important than what people are saying about themselves.

4) *Fact Listening*
We listen to people and try to remember the facts. As we do this the speaker has frequently gone on to new facts and we lost them in the process.

5) Red Flag listening

To some of us, certain words are like a red flag to a bull. When we hear them, we get upset or irritated and stop listening. These vary with individuals. However, there are various words which trigger an automatic response in some people. When this signal comes in, they tune out the speaker.

6) Interrupting

Question time in parliament is a good example. Constant interrupting does not allow the other person to speak freely. Background hubbub, noise, movement of people does not help.

Question time should be of mutual benefit to both presenter and audience. Many new presenters worry that they won't be asked any questions, and that the request 'Are there any questions?' will be met with silence. This is unusual, unless the talk is on a topic that people are just not emotionally involved in.

If it does happen, there are usually two reasons:

- You have covered all the potential questions during your presentation, or
- Your audience feels uncomfortable

Here are some ideas to overcome this situation

- Hand out question cards at the beginning of the presentation. This gives people a chance to jot down thoughts as they occur. If you ask them to do this, remind them to keep the questions short and to write clearly. This method is particularly useful for large and formal presentations.

I have seen a similar method used in small group presentations, using the flipchart. The presenter intimated that he would have a Q & A session after his presentation. He asked the group to write their questions on cards, which he would write on the flipchart during the tea break which followed. The presenter then used key words to list and group the questions. This method gave him some time to prepare answers for question time.

- Arrange with the programme chairman to select a member of the audience ahead of time to ask the first question (or ask a colleague sitting in the audience to ask a particular question), one which will elicit response from the rest of the group. Be aware that if using this method, an obviously 'rehearsed' question could lose you credibility.
- Take an information survey (which you have worked out in advance) and ask for a show of hands. The results of a simple question like 'how many of you feel we need to improve our business ethics code?' can give you new information to discuss and also gets the audience involved. This type of question can also act as an icebreaker; to start the ball rolling.
- Few people want to be first to ask a question. To get over this you could try posing your own question and answering it: 'A question I'm often asked is . . .' 'You may be wondering why my company specialises in business ethics . . .'. Try to make your question provocative. This method gives your audience food for thought, and time to think up their own questions.

Types of Questions
Overleaf are some examples of the types of questions, which you could use, and the probable outcomes.

Type of Question	Objective	Likely outcome in terms of type of information collected	Examples
1. Open-ended	To establish rapport at start of conversation	Facts, opinions	How are things? How was the traffic this morning?
	To open up a particular topic	Facts, opinions, suggestions	What ideas have you got about . . .?
	To discover their feelings	Opinions	How do you feel about . . .? What's your attitude towards . . .?
2. Closed	To collect specific pieces of information	Facts	How long have you worked for the company? What time did you arrive?
	To gain confirmation or otherwise of precise information	Facts, opinions in yes or no form	Do you agree? Is your title 'Sales Manager'?
3. Follow-up	To show interest and encourage person to continue talking	More facts, opinions and suggestions	Ah? so? and then?
	To increase the quantity and/or quality of information collected so far	More facts, opinions and suggestions and/or more perceptive insightful comments	What evidence have you? Can you tell me some more about what happened? How do you mean? Why do you say that?
	To confirm your own understanding of information collected so far	Clearer restatement of earlier facts, opinions and suggestions	So how we see it is as follows? If I've heard correctly what you are saying is?

Answering Questions

- Listen carefully to what is actually said
- Repeat. Repetition is legitimate if you feel that everyone did not hear the original question – for example if it was asked from the front of the room. It is also useful to repeat to eliminate misunderstanding. You can repeat the exact question, to check you've heard, or paraphrase, to check you have understood.
- Be courteous. Treat your audience as you would want to be treated. Use the active listening technique of giving good eye contact, nodding in agreement, and smiling when appropriate. Acknowledge their contribution with an occasional 'Thank you, that's an interesting point'. Compliment them, but only if you are sincere: 'I have enjoyed speaking with you today, you have been an excellent audience.' Adopt a polite approach, even if the question is particularly stupid and it is clear that the person has not been listening.
- Multiple questions asked as one. When asked a question with several parts, break it up and answer each part separately.
- Don't know. If you don't know the answer to a question, admit it. If you try to answer it, the audience will see through you. Rather say, 'I'm sorry I can't answer that, but I'd be happy to find out for you' (make sure you do). Make a note of the question and get back to them promptly; another way to deal with this would be to open the question up to the rest of the group: 'I'm sorry I don't know, but perhaps someone else here has the answer'. In a group of mixed backgrounds, you may have an 'expert' in the audience. One of the benefits of doing an audience profile is that you will have identified the experts in advance.

Don'ts

Defensive
Never get on the defensive, and never retaliate. No matter how rude or offensive the questioner, stay calm. If you have built up a

relationship with your audience, they will support you. I have seen a supportive audience use peer pressure to silence a hostile questioner who was intent on being heard. Later, it emerged that he had been 'requested' to attend the presentation by his manager, and was there under sufferance. This is a fairly uncommon occurrence, but it is well to be prepared – stay in control at all times.

Embarrass
Don't embarrass a questioner, even if it is clear that he has not been paying attention: 'I've covered that already, you've obviously been sleeping'; rather take the responsibility yourself: 'I'm sorry, perhaps I didn't explain that clearly.'

Public Exhibition
Never take on a person in public. This is embarrassing for everyone. Keep calm, and suggest you speak in private later. I've seen this work against a presenter, who rounded on a questioner and belittled him in front of a group of 20 colleagues. The presenter obviously believed that 'attack is the best form of defence.' This particular presenter was rather officious and arrogant, and certainly had spent no time in fostering empathy with the group beforehand. Lunch followed this incident, and it was interesting to note the body language of the group during lunch. The chastened questioner was treated to a fine display of supportive body language by his peers, whereas the presenter lunched alone.

> *Never alienate your audience – keep them with you all the way*

If you are asked a question which is clearly argumentative ask the individual to expand on his concern. You might say 'Can you tell me a little more about why you feel that way about . . .?' By keeping the would-be arguer talking, you frequently unearth hidden attitudes and agenda not evident in the question as posed.

Read Your Audience
One of the most valuable presentation skills is 'reading' an audience. If you learn what to look for, each audience will tell you how to sell your ideas to it. You can do this in many ways; examining the audience profile before the event, asking questions and mixing at registration, observing verbal and non-verbal communication. Another way is to examine key behaviours which are divided into four basic types of style: – **relator**, **socialiser**, **director** and **thinker**.

Most people display characteristics which are a mixture of several styles, but usually one particular style dominates. When you have counterchecked most of the characteristics then you can use the recommendations given.

Audience type	Characteristics	Hints on addressing them
Relators	Relatively unassertive, warm, supportive, reliable, seen as compliant, soft-hearted, slow in action and decision, avoid risky situations, want to know others' feelings, people oriented, friendly, personal, dislike interpersonal conflicts, strong counselling skills, listen actively, others feel good when close to a relator.	Show an interest in them. Ask questions at the beginning (who are you, your company? etc.). Share personal data, stories feelings and opinions. Keep eye contact, move slowly, be relaxed.
Socialisers	Creative, think quickly 'on their feet', entertainers, seek approval, persuasive, fast pace, not concerned with details, facts, spontaneous, animated, intuitive, lively, dreamers, ideas, manipulative, impetuous, excitable.	Focus on opinions, ideas, dreams, support them with stories, animation. Move fast, entertaining pace. Motivating presentations best received. Surprise them.
Directors	Firmness in relationship, productivity goals, bottom line results, stubborn, take care of others/situations, decisive in actions and decisions, extremely fast pace, high achievers, good administrators, make things happen, do many things at a time	Focus on goals, facts and graphics. Audience want to gain, to be edified. Maintain a fast pace Avoid long stories, be brief, concise. Use big pictures, avoid detail and be organised Stress the rewards. Get to the point quickly. Use assertive, powerful gestures. Show you are a competent professional.
Thinkers	Prefer a structure, sceptical, great problem solvers, poor decision makers, procrastinate decisions, persistent, systematic, may be aloof, critical, need to be right, rely on details/dates, cautious in decision making, work slowly.	Support their organised approach. Establish credibility (your qualifications). Go into details, slower pace. Facts, charts, graphs, statistics are welcomed.

Handling Objections

Whatever the merits of your idea, you can probably expect someone to present arguments as to why it should not be adopted. You should be prepared to answer these questions. The rules that apply to questions, also apply to objections. Prepare for objections in the same way as for questions. Play the devil's advocate with yourself; think of the strongest possible argument against your point of view and cover it in your presentation. If you are challenged, introduce a telling argument in the idea's favour Later, when a more positive tone has been built up again, you can refer back to the argument and neutralise it further with a few positive statements. Avoid a controversial attitude at all costs. An argumentative or defensive approach creates the impression that you are not quite sold on your own idea.

In general, you should listen, not be defensive and acknowledge the objector's point of view: 'I never thought of it like that; thank you for your thought'. When objections to your ideas are raised, you can turn them to your own advantage if you encourage the one who raised the objections to expand and elaborate. Frequently, the more one talks, the weaker the objections become. Even when the objection is irrelevant, you should stay calm. Careful listening helps you to determine whether the objection has any relevant bearing on your idea, or whether the intention is simply to reduce your stature.

Another ploy is to ask questions with which the person who raised the objection has to agree. Where applicable, a series of such questions invariably shrivels the objection and terminates in a sound conclusion with which the objector is forced to agree. This technique, of course, requires skill and much thought beforehand.

I know a successful presenter who swears by this 'three F's' technique for handling objections – feel, felt and found.

For example, answering an objection to cost:

> *I understand why you may feel that way (empathy). Many of our customers felt that way in the beginning . . . but they found that . . . (benefits gained) . . . this equipment actually saved them money in the long run (testimonial).*

This method is particularly potent if you can name a satisfied customer and cite actual benefits gained as examples.

Try not to reject objections or suggestions that would improve your idea. Even if somebody suggests something that, in your mind, would add nothing significant to your ideas, do not reject it on the spot. After you have presented your idea, arrange for a break, followed if possible by a discussion period.

The break will enable listeners to sort through various impressions and questions that occurred to them. During the final discussion period you should sum up the salient points of your ideas i.e. the anticipated benefits and advantages, the need that exists or can be created for the idea, the reasons for immediate implementation of the idea.

It is particularly important to gain the enthusiasm of those who will develop and execute your idea. If your associates and subordinates, as well as your superiors, are not convinced of its value, it may fail.

Problem Behaviour
In every group, whether it be a committee meeting, a sales presentation or a special task force in marketing, there will be some behaviour which is not productive. Here are some of the types of behaviour which you may encounter.

Dominating
Attempting to take over by excessive talking, 'pulling rank'. Can occur when manager and subordinates attend the presentation. Seniority often predominates.

Blocking
Any action which interferes with the progress of the group. Examples of this include deliberately getting off the topic; recounting personal experiences which are irrelevant to the topic; rejecting the ideas of others; and taking a negative approach, insisting that nothing can be done. 'We tried that before and it didn't solve the problem'.

Aggression
Occurs when a member blames others for his own mistakes. Showing hostility to individuals or groups (company), attaching motives to others. Deflating self-image of others. 'If you had completed the report on schedule we would have won the order.'

Withdrawing
Opposite of aggression. People withdraw from the group by exhibiting such non-participating behaviour as day-dreaming, doodling or gazing out of the window.

Seeking Status
Drawing attention by boasting, talking in an aggressive manner, distracting dress or mannerisms:
'At . . . we always do it this way.'

Special Pleading
Going 'all out' to get a point across. Often this person will have hidden motives or hobby horses. These are often used to cloud the issue and to support their point of view:
'All my divisional directors'; 'The average woman manager.'

Manipulating
Attempting to control the group by pulling strings or rank. Frequently resort to blatant flattery, name-dropping. Tend to divide the group into cliques.

Distracting
Diverting attention from the task in hand. A distracting person very often comes late, interrupts others, gets off the topic. Generally non-productive behaviour.

Confession
Using the group for personal catharsis. The 'confessor' seeks sympathy or pity for personal mistakes, feelings or beliefs irrelevant to the group task. Heard recently at a presentation: Presenter,

pointing to error on overhead slide: 'I must apologise for this mistake, my secretary can't spell.'

Rationalising
Explaining failure or inadequacy by finding some unsubstantial excuse for the failure: 'Sorry the report is not finished, I've been on holiday for the past two weeks.'

These types of behaviour can be found in most large groups of people. They may emerge in your audience as:

The know-it-alls
To handle: Ask them questions to involve them and allow them to share their experiences and knowledge.

The Monopolisers
To handle: Ask someone else 'What do you think?' or say to the monopoliser: 'Let's hear someone else's opinion.' Use your body language to ignore them – stand side on to them instead of face on, and withdraw eye contact.

The Nitpickers
To handle: Give their detailed questions back to them to answer, or to group. For example, listen to the question and then put it to the group, saying 'How do others here handle the situation?'

The Timid
To handle timid people ask them open-ended questions. Reinforce any participation with a warm 'thank-you'. Shy people may feel afraid or insecure in a large group. Perhaps talk to them during the break; they need reassurance.

The Show-Offs
To handle: Draw attention to them. Ask them to repeat their comments to everyone. Politely remind them of time limitations: 'We only have ten minutes until coffee, let's talk about it then.'

QUESTION TIME

The Attackers

To handle: Recognise the attack. Don't take it personally or be defensive. Humour often works here.

Questions and Answer Checklist

- Anticipate and prepare possible questions and objections. (Check your audience profile.)
- Truly listen. This is an essential skill for a successful presenter.
- Maintain your credibility and control
- Stay calm at all times – don't be defensive
- Treat your audience as individuals
- Welcome questions; be warm and friendly
- Give the audience full attention – display positive body language
- Answer the questions briefly and stop
- Give the questioner 80% eye contact, 20% to the rest of the audience
- Recognise questions in order. When more than one questioner has his hand up – mentally note the first, and deal with the others in order.
- Initially direct questions to the whole group (shotgun approach), follow with questions to individuals (rifle approach). This avoids putting listeners on the spot.

12. Finding Your Style

If you are going to work with colleagues and customers by facilitating the discovery of their needs, problems and solutions, you must first understand yourself.

Customers make the purchasing decisions and thus it is to our benefit to treat them the way they prefer. For that reason, we need to observe the golden rule of selling. 'Sell the customer the way he would like to be sold' and not the way you would like to sell.

Behavioural Styles
Unlike your thoughts, feelings and emotions, which can be hidden from others, your behaviour is observable. Research shows that there are a variety of observable social styles. Most people can operate successfully by combining several styles, but usually one style will dominate.

How often have you 'hit it off' with a customer or client almost from the first minute you meet? Or, conversely, have felt uncomfortable in their presence, not quite being able to work out why there is a problem?

This latter situation can often happen even when the presenter has followed all the rules of good preparation. In a selling situation, the most successful sales people are those, who as well as thorough preparation, are aware of their own behavioural style, and that of their prospect. Compatibility and 'hitting it off' often happens as a result of matching behaviour.

Behavioural researchers have isolated three characteristics of human behaviour which, when combined, describe styles of behaviour.

Assertiveness
The individual's effort to influence the thoughts and actions of others.

Responsiveness
The individual's tendency to respond to others or events with a show of feeling or lack of inhibition.

Affiliation
The individual's tendency to value the ideas, opinions and company of others.

For the purpose of this exercise only two of the styles, assertiveness and responsiveness, will be used.

There are four major behavioural styles. Each one approaches a problem differently. If we know our own style and are able to recognise the styles of others, we should be able to interact more effectively with them.

Our basic style is our own most comfortable mode of behaving. You can get a general impression of your particular style with the following techniques:

Assertiveness: Read the brief descriptions and decide which ones would be selected by your peers to describe you. How would they say you act most of the time?

Low Assertiveness (ask)

- easygoing; unimposing on others
- asks questions and listens, but may not talk unless there is a specific reason to do so.
- passive orientation; conservative
- acts slowly; decides slowly; tentative- relaxed; accepts control; avoids risk

High Assertiveness (tell)

- ambitious; likes to know what is going on and takes action to find out.
- talks a lot with others, even when it may not be his or her business to do so.
- active orientation; risk taker
- decides quickly; competitive
- resists control; takes charge; opinionated

Responsiveness: read the brief descriptions and decide which ones would be selected by your peers to describe you. How would they say you act most of the time?

Low Responsiveness (control)

- self-sufficient; independent of others
- tends to be formal; controlled; cautious with feelings
- thinking-oriented; discusses facts
- businesslike; reserved; seems hard to get to know
- precise; specific; task oriented
- efficient with time
- guarded, cautious in communication
- rational in decision-making, self-discipline
- demanding of others and self

High Responsiveness (emote)

- self indulgent, involved with others
- tends to be casual, fun loving, and open with feelings
- feeling-oriented; discusses opinions
- permissive; warm; approachable
- informal; unreserved; people-oriented
- impulsive; communicative; dramatic
- undisciplined about time
- informal in speech and dress

- decision-making by emotion
- friendly; personal; seems easy to get to know.

This is an enlightening exercise to do as a group activity. It is interesting to hear how you come across to others. Often we present a completely different face to the world from what we imagine. We may have behavioural traits which hinder good communications. Polishing up on these could mean the difference between a good presentation and a superb one, a successful sale or a failure.

Try now to determine where you think you would fit. The combinations of assertiveness and responsiveness are shown below:

Low Assertiveness and Low Responsiveness = Analytical
Low Assertiveness and High Responsiveness = Amiable
High Assertiveness and Low Responsiveness = Driver
High Assertiveness and High Responsiveness = Expressive

Note: There are no good and bad styles. No one is better than the others.

The following are 'shorthand' descriptions of each of the four styles as they are perceived by others:

DRIVER

Determined, requiring, thorough, dominating, decisive, severe, aggressive, efficient, tough-minded.

EXPRESSIVE

Personable, enthusiastic, stimulating, dramatic, gregarious, excitable, promotional, undisciplined.

AMIABLE

Responsive, easy going, accepting, dependable, complying, retiring, supportive, respectful, agreeable, dependent, emotional, conforming.

ANALYTICAL

Industrious, persistent, serious, exacting, vigilant, critical, orderly, indecisive, impersonal, independent.

The secret of good communication is to know your strengths and weaknesses. This is the advantage of using a video when rehearsing. Strengths can be identified and used to advantage, whereas weaknesses can be identified and improved.

Strengths and Weaknesses
Each style has special strengths and weaknesses:

Drivers are strong in solving problems and are weak in the amiable strengths. Drivers can be effective, but other people find them stressful.

Drivers need to listen more

Expressives are strong in persuading others and are weak in the analyticals' strengths. Expressives can be very effective, but tend to speak before analysing a situation.

Expressives need to think before speaking

Amiables are strong in understanding and weak in the drivers' strengths. Often they are the 'glue' which holds a group together.

Amiables need to procrastinate less

Analyticals are strong in understanding the situation and are weak in the expressives' strengths. They make thorough decisions.

Analyticals need to procrastinate less

Each of the styles can be successful, relate well to other people, and attain great personal growth and happiness. And, in fact, studies show the population of salespeople is equally distributed in all styles.

One thing to keep in mind when considering the different styles is that your behaviour may be interpreted differently by different people.

For example:

Style	Behaviour	Could be seen as
Analytical	Serious Orderly Careful	Reserved Structured Indecisive
Driver	Determined Decisive Getting things done	Stubborn Tough Dominating
Amiable	Agreeable Willing Supportive	Ingratiating Conforming Dependent

Controlling Situations

In controlling situations involving each of the four styles:

Drivers are seen as assertive, impersonal, and task-oriented. They control the situation using authority and proof.

Expressives are seen as assertive, personal and people-oriented. They control the situation using ideas and emotion.

Amiables are seen as nonassertive, personal and people-oriented. They keep situations comfortable by being pleasant and agreeable.

Analyticals are seen as non assertive, impersonal and task oriented. They keep situations efficient by being thorough.

Problem Solving

In problem solving discussions:

Drivers would probably talk the most and, if they formed an opinion, work the hardest to influence the decision, using facts and reason to back their opinion. They probably would listen the least.

Expressives are as stimulating as possible, and they may become bored with lengthy consideration of details. They tend to want to decide quickly, and may make an emotional appeal to the others to go along with their opinions.

Amiables listen more, seem willing to go along with group opinion, state their ideas as opinions when asked, and give in rather than argue. They are often easy to like and give cohesion to a group. They are easy to deal with and generally have a special value to a group by being able to smooth over conflicts.

Analyticals also listen. They have thoughtful opinions which reflect an attempt to analyse the situation thoroughly. Their comments may be lengthy and precise, even though they don't demand to be heard.

13. Other Types of Presentations

IMPROMPTU SPEAKING

'And now . . . would you like to take a few minutes and give us your view on . . .'

These words can put the fear of death into most people, but this is a common request heard at staff and board meetings. As you hear your name, your heart beats faster, your mind goes blank.

'Thinking on your feet' is not as difficult as it may seem if you can master a few guidelines that also apply to the prepared speech.

First, quickly formulate the general purpose of your talk. What are your objectives – are you going to ask for action, inform, persuade? Next, consider your listeners' objectives. Use the simple prompts, who, why, where, when and how, to build up your talk. Do they need more data – if so, what? Should they feel differently – how? Should they take action – when? After deciding your objective, choose some mental prompts which consist of your key words. You could build on the previous speaker's comments or briefly summarise what has been said and add your own comments.

EXTEMPORANEOUS SPEAKING

The impromptu speech is given 'on the spur of the moment' usually without any preparation time. On the other hand, the extemporaneous speech is one which appears spontaneous, but in fact has actually been prepared. Winston Churchill was a master of this technique. Apparently his colleagues often heard him practise his 'impromptu speeches: 'Honourable Members, I did not intend to say this in the House today . . .'

For most people it is extremely difficult to memorise a presentation and then to present it word for word extemporaneously. There is a constant danger that if you forget one key word, you will lose your ideas, continuity and spontaneity. One way of overcoming this is to learn to speak from ideas alone – from personal experience and knowledge, then the words will come. If you have a good memory, you can memorise the general outline of the presentation, and a few key words on a card should suffice.

Both the impromptu and extemporaneous presentation should include the other vital ingredients to make them a success: enthusiasm and vitality.

The Lecture

This is a popular method of presentation when large groups of people are involved. The presenter or lecturer is imparting information to the audience. There are certain advantages in this method of presentation:

- It is an effective way to present material to large groups.
- It can be used to give the outline or background to a very broad subject, of which the details can be given later by other presentation techniques; for example, in small group presentations, discussion groups, using supporting material such as reports and papers.

The disadvantages are:

- The audience are not involved. If the presenter does not actively attempt to keep the attention level high, then the audience will lose interest. This is made more difficult because of the volume of information which is being presented.

Other Types of Presentations

- There is no feedback. The presenter does not know if he is on the right track, or if the audience is taking in the information being put across.

Hints for lecture presentation:

- Know your objectives and those of your audience
- Research your audience and your material
- Have a clear lecture structure
- Hook the audience attention in the opening and emphasise the key points.
- Tell them what's in it for them
- Check that your verbals and non-verbals match. Be enthusiastic and positive.
- Be aware of audience non-verbal communication. Look for signs of restlessness, boredom. Be prepared to change your pace if necessary.
- Maintain interest by including humour, anecdotes, examples, visuals as appropriate.
- Summarise frequently.
- End on a positive note.

Decide which visual aids are most suitable for the size of audience. A lectern is useful for holding notes. Have a full dress rehearsal, checking all equipment. If someone is working your audio visuals, check the cues with them.

The word 'lecture' conjures up unhappy memories for many people: hours of boredom listening to experts extol the virtues of their particular theory; the university professor reading his latest paper. It doesn't have to be that way. More than any other type of presentation, the lecture to large audiences takes on the aura of a theatrical event: everything should be slightly more exaggerated, the voice, the gestures. Keep it lively – and keep them interested.

Presenting a Paper

This can present certain problems. Is it a presentation or a reading? You will of course be required to follow the normal practice of the organising body, but otherwise, I suggest that you tackle this as you would a business presentation.

Firstly, prepare a presentation. Use your preparation checklist for this. Follow the advice on structure, delivery, visual aids. Gather together all the material on your subject. Go through every document, reference, item of correspondence. Retrace the whole project from inception to completion and check all your facts. This will refresh your memory. You will be surprised at how much detail you had forgotten.

When you have completed the presentation, have a rehearsal. When you are happy with the finished result, start on your own paper. You have now done most of the work, so writing the paper should be relatively easy. You have a shape in mind, you have reviewed the relevant materials and you have prepared what you are going to say, in conversational style. Your preparation, enthusiasm, and knowledge will be evident to your audience and they will respond by sitting up and taking notice.

The Technical Presentation

Technical professionals are often let down by poor presentation skills. They may be highly talented and knowledgeable in technical areas, but are often overtaken in promotion by less efficient colleagues who present well and project what management sees as the right image. It is important for technical professionals to be exposed to other groups. High visibility can also be extremely useful in gathering support for technical ideas.

As well as adhering to the general rules for presentation preparation, the technical specialist needs to take particular care when deciding what level of detail is required by the audience. All too often the technical presentation can sink in a morass of technical detail and jargon.

Other Types of Presentations

Examine your audience carefully; for example, you may be asked to give an informative talk to the local Chamber of Commerce on the latest information technology. Although your audience will consist of intelligent business people, don't assume that they know even the basics about the subject. Simple words that are common in the world of computing and communications are not always understood by the general public. Another audience may be a gathering of technical staff. You may be part of a group presentation, where you provide the technical expertise. Here you can go into more detail.

In every instance, technical presentations should be delivered at a level of understanding that is comfortable for your listeners. If you talk above or below their level of understanding they will stop listening.

Very often, the technical presentation will include a product demonstration. Give the demonstration rehearsal as much time and effort as the rest of the presentation. Check everything and thoroughly review your 'What if . . .' list.

When giving the presentation to non-technical groups:

- Briefly explain any technical jargon which you will use.
- Encourage questions throughout the presentation. This will enable the audience to clarify any points that are unclear.
- Keep the information short and punchy. Give the minimum of detail to meet your objectives.
- Allow a reasonable length of time for questions at the end.

Competitive Presentations

Professional services are offered by a growing number of consultants, many of whom are women starting up in business for the first time. We live in competitive times and the nature of the consultancy business means that time is money. The simple format of *preparation, professionalism and persistence* will help formulate your approach.

1) Preparation

This stage should be very familiar to you by now. Time and effort spent beforehand is the rule. Whilst it is not realistic to expect to win them all, careful planning will provide a better strike rate.

There are growing numbers of professional competitors in all the market sectors, eager for business. Very often initial meetings with clients and the process that follows are conducted in parallel with others. This first meeting is important to demonstrate professional competence. If this initial contact is not favourable, then you may not get the opportunity for further discussion.

Clients themselves are increasingly demanding. They do not assume that the first person to walk through the door is fine to appoint, nor do they regard the relationship once started, as 'for life'. They expect the consultant to understand their business, their market, and their problems.

Let's imagine that you, as a consultant, have made an initial appointment to meet a prospective client. Here is a checklist to help you think through your strategy:

- Gather together all the information on the company before the first meeting: information by telephone, company reports, sales literature.
- Know who you will be talking to at the meeting and their position with the company, their role in the decision-making process. Ask if they are speaking with other consultants. Clients are very often quite open about this information.
- Try to define the objectives i.e. what the client is looking for. At the initial sage this is often difficult to define, but you will have at least a general idea. Look for connections. How might you be able to help? Any recommendations? Are there areas that require clarification?
- Be prepared to take along some of your own work, literature, case histories, success record, which show your professionalism (often referred to as intrinsic selling).
- Personal presentation: Remember you are the company you present – sell yourself. (See chapter 9.)

Professionalism

In demonstrating professionalism, it is important that we distinguish between 'the professional salesman' and the professional who can sell. In most cases, clients are looking for the latter. Creativity and a professional approach are crucial for success. This must be apparent to the client from the beginning or they will not take the matter further.

Show an interest in the company. Ask questions and make it clear that you have done your homework. Use questioning techniques to elicit information, which will help you identify the root problem as soon as possible. Show a grasp and understanding of the client's actual situation and in the early stages make a 'pass' at a solution to demonstrate competence. Agree on the next stage, which is likely to be a written proposal from you.

Use a systematic approach. Put as much effort into this stage as you would into a formal presentation. Research and prepare thoroughly. The written proposal should look and read well: use clear language and focus on the client, identifying the present situation, making the proposal and outlining the benefits to the client.

Persistence

Success in part goes to those who are persistent, who follow up confidently and who, when successful, maintain a good client relationship.

Successful Proposals

The initial meeting with your prospective client is an opportunity for discussion and information gathering. If this meeting is successful you may be asked to put your proposal in writing, or, you may be asked back to present it.

Here are some pointers to maximise your chances of successful proposals and pitches:

- Put yourself in your clients' shoes. During your preparation ask yourself: 'What will influence them?'

- Decide when you will present the written proposal.

  – Either send it before the presentation *or*
  – Give it out when you begin the presentation so that your audience can refer to it *or*
  – Give it out after the presentation.

It is a matter of choice how you decide to handle the proposal. It will vary according to your audience, the occasion and the complexity of the material you are presenting.

- Keep the written proposal brief and to the point.
- References are often required by the client. It is a good idea to have some written references available, or you could offer contact names. (Make sure you have their agreement.)
- Take your audience through the proposal. Give an overview – describe key elements in detail – summarise. This is a suitable format if the audience have it in front of them. If they have already seen it, then add your comments and take questions.
- If you are presenting to a small group around a table, consider using visuals. The display board (see chapter on visual aids) is excellent for this purpose.
- Remember to include all the elements of successful presentation in your pitch. Anticipate and have prepared approximate work/completion timescales as well as an estimate of your fees.

Addressing a Foreign Audience

Here are some tips on speaking to foreign groups.
If you have the luxury of an interpreter:

- Make sure you practise together
- Break up the material into clear sections so that one idea or thought can be translated.

Remember that this method will double the length of your speech.

Address the audience, not the interpreter (all the rules for eye contact are still relevant here).

More and more presentations are being given to foreign groups whose first language is not English. Many people in your audience will have some understanding of English. In this case:

- It is a nice gesture if you can say at least a few words of welcome to guests in their language.
- If possible, allow for some tuning-in time, where the listeners can tune in to your voice, your intonation and your accent. One way to do this is during coffee or registration time. If this is not possible, then allow a few minutes at the beginning of the presentation – perhaps when you are welcoming them to the event.
- Use short words and sentences. Many foreigners have a higher level of proficiency in reading English than they have in the spoken language. When teaching English to foreign groups, to maximise understanding, I found it invaluable to speak clearly, giving them time to digest the information, and also limit the amount of information given, for example one idea per sentence. If you give them too much information too soon, they will go into confusion overload. On the other hand if it is poorly paced they will lose interest.
- Use simple language, avoid clichés, jargon and technical terms.

Research at a number of institutions in both the UK and USA shows that approximately 78 per cent of the English language, as it is used in daily life, is composed of active sentence structures. For example 'We recorded (active verb) a show of hands' instead of 'A show of hands was recorded' (passive verb).

Even if presenting to a technical or specialist audience, never assume they understand the jargon or buzz words. Try to cut these out as much as possible. If you must use them, then check audience understanding. For example, 'Do you all understand what I mean when I say?' . . . or at the beginning – 'If I use any technical terms which are not familiar to you, please let me know, and I'll explain them as we go along.'

CHAIRMANSHIP

At some time in your career you may be asked to chair a meeting. Part of this will mean that you introduce other speakers. Alternatively you, as a speaker, may be introduced by him.

Firstly, what qualities should a competent chairman have?

1. Control

You must exercise control – without appearing to dominate. Part of your job is to protect the speaker against interruption; you are the host, particularly to the speaker, generally to the audience. You are the liaison officer between them.

2. Dignity

You must show quiet dignity

3. Humour

A sense of humour is an asset. Think about the speaker in the House of Commons. By a shrewdly timed intervention he or she can defuse a difficult situation and regain control.

4. Authority

Control is important for the chairman. You should keep calm and even tempered at all times.

5. Competent Speaker

A chairman should be a competent speaker. The tone of the meeting can be set by your opening remarks – by what you say and how you say it. It is in the opening remarks that the chairman can help a nervous speaker.

6. Brevity

Keep your opening remarks and instructions brief.

7. Speakers

Before the event, the chairman should arrange with the speakers how things like questions will be handled.

8. Introductions

Many nervous speakers have divulged presentation material to the chairman. I have been in the position where a chatty chairman has pre-empted most of my material. As a chairman, check your introduction with the speaker. As a speaker, give the chairman only the information he needs to introduce you. And to avoid overlap it's a good idea for a speaker to type out his own introduction and give this to the chairperson in advance.

9. Seating

For a large audience, seating will probably be theatre style, with a raised platform for the speakers. If you have more than four others on the platform with you, a simple diagram showing the seating arrangements is useful. It is customary for the speaker to be on the chairman's right. If there is more than one speaker, then they alternate, right and left.

10. Timing

Always start the meeting in good time. If delays seems advisable – for example if a coach bringing a large group has broken down but is now under way – or the speaker has been delayed, take the audience into your confidence, and suggest with their permission that you delay the start time. Your audience will appreciate being put in the picture, and will be sympathetic.

11. Introductions

In introducing the speaker mention only those points which add weight to his authority to speak on his subject. If possible don't read out facts about the speaker but memorize them.
    An introduction should only last between one and three minutes.
    Be conversational, speak just as you would to a friend.
    Call on the speaker by name. Don't forget his name and have to search notes looking for it. Also check pronunciation of unusual names.

12. Control Time

If you are chairing several speakers, be aware of timing. Advise the speakers beforehand that, for example, you will pass them a card, (written in large clear lettering) when, say, three minutes remain. As chairman you are responsible for ensuring that all speakers have the time allotted to them.

13. Active Listening

Be aware of your body language – give the speaker eye contact now and again, also glance at the audience and look interested.

14. Question Time

If possible call a short break before question time.
    Either have a couple of questions to hand yourself or arrange with someone in the audience to ask one. This is useful if there is no immediate response to 'any questions?'

Request that members keep questions to the point. (For example, '... so that we may have as many good questions as possible ...')

15. Closing

Either the chairman thanks the speaker, or, with a linked sentence of thanks, he will call on a member to do so. The vote of thanks should be brief. It is also a nice idea to select one or two points from the speech and underline them. After a polite vote of thanks, you can cheerfully declare the meeting closed.

LEADING DYNAMIC MEETINGS

Besides individual presentations, another form of public speaking you may get involved in is discussion groups or meetings. You are not in the spotlight as you are when giving presentations, but rather your success depends on your ability to facilitate everyone else's interaction.

Your ability to lead effective meetings can either enhance or detract from your career advancement. They are just like any other organisational resources – they require careful preparation and discipline.

Many business meetings take place out of habit, the weekly staff meeting, the monthly board meeting. Meetings mean time. Whether that time is productive or wasted depends on you, the leader. Meetings cost companies, in terms of direct salaries: preparation costs; psychological costs, such as the low morale resulting from a poorly-run meeting; and opportunity costs; such as the work people could be doing instead of attending the meeting.

Here are some simple guidelines to follow in planning for meetings:

1. Consider whether or not a meeting is the answer. If you merely want to inform the attendees of something, would a memo be

more efficient? or perhaps discussion issues one-on-one with key people is an alternative. You should not call a meeting if:

- Key people are not available
- Phone calls or written communication will suffice
- There is insufficient preparation time
- The cost is too high

2. Decide your specific objectives. Do you want to:

- Inform or explain? Meetings are excellent vehicles to provide information regarding plans or programmes because you can put your personality into them, something you cannot do in a memo. These 'information dumps' are mainly one-way, with time allowed to clarify questions but not for thorough discussion of the issues presented. This type of meeting is more effective when participants are given written material to support what is said.
- Train? Meetings can be specifically called to teach participants something, or to turn plans into positive action by letting people know what to do and how to do it. These are more difficult than other meeting forms because you expect others to leave knowing what you know and being able to do it. And this requires practice.
- Seek information? Meetings are a vehicle to gather opinions or reach a quick consensus. If you must resolve an issue by asking for a show of hands, do it!
- Problem solve? Meetings serve to collect various experiences and opinions, which may lead to the solution to a problem. If you lead a brainstorming session, make certain that you handle it effectively.
- Persuade? Use meetings to present your ideas to those people ultimately responsible for executing them. Be careful in this type of meeting to have thoroughly analysed your participants. Start with a question-and-discussion period on your topic to get a feel for the group's viewpoints.

- Regardless of your objective, be able to answer this question before your meeting:

  'At the end of this meeting . . . will have been accomplished'

3. Decide who should attend the meeting

Effectiveness can decrease as your meeting size increases, so give serious thought to who should attend. Perhaps some people need only be present for part of the meeting. Also consider whether they need any background information beforehand.

4. Prepare an Agenda

Try to distribute it a few days before the meeting. Informal agendas written on a flip chart fit the informal style of many meetings, and while they do not give everyone time to consider the topics in advance, they do keep the meeting on target. Labelling items for 'discussion' or 'decision' will help clarify them.

5. Select the appropriate facilities, equipment and time for the meeting. Assign someone to take minutes, writing down action items, and distributing them afterwards. Also evaluate the session if you feel the need for feedback.

Brainstorming

We talked briefly about this in the presentation preparation stage. It is particularly useful and can be incorporated into most decision-making formats by following some simple guidelines.

Four Basic Rules

1. List all ideas or alternatives in a central location
2. No questions or discussion regarding ideas
3. No judgement of ideas, criticism or complaints
4. Allow repetition of ideas

It is best to select a recorder who writes down all ideas, whether they seem valuable or not. Many times, poor ideas serve a useful purpose. For example, humorous ones break tension. They can make other people feel more at ease about offering their own suggestions. Seemingly poor ideas also serve as springboards for more practical ones.

Fifteen to twenty minutes is the optimum time to allow for getting ideas out, and three to seven people the best number for brainstorming. Fewer than three people may result in too quick an exploration of ideas, whereas more than seven can result in some participants feeling lost or unnecessary – therefore remaining silent.

After all ideas have been listed, the next phase of brainstorming is determining the merit of each one in a general sense. Ideas that are totally off-base should now be discounted; however by waiting until this phase, the group has probably forgotten which ideas belong to which participant. In this way, the group can become more task oriented.

The next step is to generate all possible advantages and disadvantages for the remaining ideas. You may even want to use a structural rating scale. Taking a break at this time in the meeting is conducive to this process, because it allows people to step back from the situation for a moment and return with a refreshed perspective.

Finally, do not try to force the group to arrive at a single solution. Your session may end with two or three best alternatives – and a new session could pick up from there.

Meeting Handouts

Handouts are an excellent supplement to any meeting. To maximise your participants' effectiveness, have a written agenda or schedule in front of them. This provides them with some direction; they will know exactly how much of their time will be spent and can make sure that they really do belong there. Distribute agendas or schedules before your meeting starts. They give prompt people something to look at while you are waiting for late arrivals. If you choose to use other reference handouts, make them uniform in size, because:

1) It is not easy to find material or carry it around if it is in different shapes.
2) It may be information that participants will copy to circulate within their own departments.

Agenda

When producing the agenda, certain standard items are usually included.

Any apologies for absence are usually mentioned and noted before the start of business. If the meeting is one of a series, approval of the minutes or notes of the previous meeting will be needed. At formal and semi-formal meetings, the chair will then sign the minutes. Any matters arising from the minutes which are not somewhere else on the agenda can then be raised. Items are then listed; the order may depend on importance, with items of most importance early on. Routine items such as correspondence etc. are usually dealt with early on, to get them out of the way.

A good agenda will not just list the titles of items, but will indicate what each should achieve. It may also indicate who is to lead the discussion or, in formal meetings, who is to propose a motion. It will be supported by any papers or reports as necessary. For example:

Agenda

1. Apologies for absence
2. Notes of meeting of 7/8/92
3. Budget update
   All divisional directors to report (reports attached)
4. Departmental Reports
   Communications Group Manager to report on attitude survey (initial survey figures attached)
5. New product development

discussion of new addition to 101 range
led by B. Allen, Research and Development
6. Any other business
7. Date of next meeting
Bill Bradley (in the chair)

Staff Meetings
If meetings are going to be held at a certain time each week there should be business to conduct. The advantage of regular staff meetings is that participants can keep this time free. Make sure, however, that your staff meetings all have a clear objective so they will be time well spent.

This means planning a preliminary agenda and distributing it to all participants. Participants should be encouraged to study this agenda and suggest other items to incorporate into the final one.

The success of the meeting will depend largely on the person leading it. Many companies 'rotate' the chairman's role. This provides an opportunity for each manager to practise his management skills.

In this case, the last item on the agenda (date of next meeting) would be followed by the name of the next person elected to be 'chairman'.

Are Minutes Necessary?
The main purpose of minutes taking are to provide:-

- A permanent account of points discussed
- A record of the decisions taken
- An indication of further action

Minutes can vary in their detail from a highly formal word by word account of a meeting e.g. *Hansard*, to a brief set of notes on decisions taken. The halfway stage records the question, the questioner, the answer, the answerer, but omits the discussion between raising the question and getting the final answer. For most meetings the appropriate type of minutes are informal. These fulfil the two purposes of recording decisions and providing information

Other Types of Presentations

on future action, which is often all that is needed. The minutes can be written in the form of brief, clear notes. It is important to remember, however, that clarity should not be sacrificed to brevity. If a member of the meeting wants some contribution minuted in detail, this must be done.

Why should We Take Minutes?

People often shy clear of minutes taking because they feel it is a difficult task. This need not be the case. With informal minutes taking, the interested member of a meeting is likely to be taking mental minutes of the proceedings, noting what is discussed and the decision – after all he is part of the decision making process! It requires only a little extra effort to translate the mental notes to brief written notes while the meeting progresses. It may force him to double check his understanding of what is happening at the meeting, which is beneficial to himself and probably to other members also. In meetings with a smaller number of people the chairman may take the minutes himself, but it is a better use of resources if another member does so. The simpler the form of the minutes the better, provided this is consistent with clarity.

Meeting Planner

When you are involved in a meeting with one or more other people, the effectiveness of the meeting will depend not only on the extent to which you are able to be skilful in your interactions with others, but also on the strategy which you adopt for the meeting. Even the most skilful person is unlikely to achieve his desired objectives unless his strategy is sound. Here is a checklist of points to consider when planning a meeting.

Meeting Planner Checklist

1. Who is it that you are trying to influence? (Who do you need to persuade – who really makes the decision?)
2. Who else will/should be there? (Who can be your ally? Or who will be putting a different point of view?)

3. Where will the meeting be held? (A meeting on another's home territory is likely to increase his sense of security. Meeting on your territory is likely to reduce the other's sense of security.)
4. Will it be a special meeting/an accidental meeting/or tacked on to some other business?
5. What is your time strategy? Are you going to achieve what you want in one meeting or do you need to plan a series of meetings?
6. How will you open the meeting? (You will need to get a contract with the other person.)
7. Will you reveal your position or draw out the other's position? How much of the 'air time' will you use?
8. What is the crunch point of the meeting? How will you deal with it?
9. If all goes well, what do you want them to say at the end of the meeting?
10. How will you close the meeting? (You will need to get a contract where everyone is clear about what they need to do and when.)

Leading Group Discussions

Often the most effective speakers have a knack for interacting with their group. This skill can also contribute to your success as a discussion group. Any question following a speech can really be thought of an an interactive system.

A	B	C
Individual Contributions: Talents Abilities Enthusiasm *Group:* Goals Expectations *External:* Group size Meeting Location	Interaction Communication – alters attitudes	Outputs Decisions Attitude Changes Rewards

(with + between A and B, and + between B and C)

Other Types of Presentations

By looking at a meeting or discussion as an interactive system, with you at the controls, we should be better able to explain why some are more pleasant and productive than others.

Only to a certain extent can you be responsible for the inputs themselves. You can, however, clarify group goals. Make sure that everyone understands what their role is and establish the right climate in the room by having the right seating arrangement, equipment and so on.

Possibly the most difficult aspect of modifying group inputs is balancing participants' discussion within the time and structure you have allotted.

These three general guidelines will assist you:

1. Organise discussion around a specific result (objective).
2. Prepare so that you know what result you expect to receive.
3. Control the inputs by allowing a free flow that is guided towards your predetermined result. The discussion may otherwise be unproductive. ('If you don't know where you're going . . .')

Here is a list of special skills needed for successful discussion control:

Starting Skills

- Crystallising issues mentally before beginning
- Getting attention
- Starting individual talking
- Stating points and problems clearly
- Announcing agenda items
- Asking good questions
- Focusing on one issue at a time
- Drawing people out
- Encouraging contributions

Once you have the group involved, it is up to you as the leader to signpost and guide the discussion along the pre-determined route.

Guiding Skills

- Listening
- Silence – pauses
- Reading body language
- Sensing and adjusting to moods
- Following agendas
- Clarifying meanings
- Steering discussion towards goal
- Introducing relevant new points into discussion
- Balancing inputs – equal member participation
- Managing conflict
- Always remaining neutral

The main aim at this stage is to guide the discussion whilst allowing maximum group participation in relation to the objectives and agreed timescales.

Stopping Skills

- Summarising
- Acknowledging what people have said
- Knowing when to recap
- Ensuring that each participant gets to finish
- Controlling individuals who are talking at the wrong time
- Protecting individuals from attack by other group members
- Building consensus

When leading meetings and discussions it is useful for the leader to recognise the roles that people play in these situations. Many of the roles can make positive contributions to a meeting, others can block progress and inhibit participation of other members of the group. A good leader should recognise and utilise the positive roles and also recognise and deal with the 'blockers'.

Anticipation and avoidance preparation will go a long way in dealing with these role players.

Roles people play in meetings

Group Blocking Roles

The aggressor	Criticises and deflates status of others; disagrees with others aggressively
The blocker	Stubbornly disagrees; rejects others' views; cites unrelated personal experiences; returns to topics already resolved
The withdrawer	Won't participate; wool gatherer; converses privately; self-appointed note-taker
The recognition seeker	Boasts; excessive talking; conscious of his status
The topic jumper	Continually changes subject
The dominator	Tries to take over, assert authority, manipulate group
The special-interest pleader	Uses group's time to plead his own case
The playboy	Wastes group's time showing off; story teller; nonchalant; cynical
The self-confessor	Talks irrelevantly about his own feelings and insights
The devil's advocate	More devil than advocate

Group Maintenance Roles

The tension reliever	Uses humour or calls for break at appropriate times to draw off negative feelings
The compromiser	Willing to yield when necessary for progress
The harmoniser	Mediates differences; reconciles points of view
The encourager	Praises and supports others; friendly; encouraging.

The gate keeper	Keeps communication open; encourages participation.

Group Building Roles

The initiator	Suggests new or different ideas for discussion and approaches to problems
The opinion giver	States pertinent beliefs about discussion at others' suggestions
The elaborator	Builds on suggestions of others
The clarifier	Gives relevant examples; offers rationales; probes for meaning and understanding; restates problems
The tester	Raises questions to test out whether group is ready to come to a decision
The summariser	Reviews discussion; pulls it together

Media Interviews

There can be any number of reasons why you may be approached to take part in an interview on radio or television. You may be asked because you are the chairman or spokesman for a company or organisation, or as an expert on a newsworthy subject.

You may be given very short notice before an interview; however, it is worth doing as much preparation as time allows.

Firstly, you must decide if you want to take part. Here are some questions to ask yourself before you accept:

- What can I expect to get out of it?
- What are the benefits to my company?
- Am I the best person to be interviewed?
- Have I sufficient preparation time?
- Do the interviewers/media have a good reputation?
- What if I say no?

Other Types of Presentations

On the last point, remember that if you refuse, you may have to balance the effects of giving an unconvincing interview against the reaction to 'A spokesman for X company refused to comment.'

If you decide to say yes, you can then start on your preparation.

Here is a checklist to help you think through this stage:

Preparation

Questions to ask

Will the interview be live or pre-recorded?

Live interviews are more nerve-racking than pre-recorded ones. Pre-recorded interviews will be edited. Generally, editing will improve how you sound, for example any hesitancy in answering can be cut out.

Who will be conducting the interview?

This is an important point, as it may give some clues as to how the interview will be handled. Keep in mind that interviewers are like chairmen, and should treat all sides equally whatever their personal views. They should question on behalf of the general public.

Will the interviewers be supporting or attacking your point of view?

Make sure that the radio or television station has a correct impression of your viewpoint. Ask some questions to assess their approach.

How long will it last?

Remember the key points you want to get across, particularly if you have only a short time to express your views.

When and where will the interview take place?

Check that you have accurate details and instructions on directions. Re-confirm time and place the day before.

Will you be told questions in advance?

Often interviewees are given a list of possible questions. This is very helpful and assists you in formulating the most appropriate response. Try to compose short and concise answers. If you are not given advance warning of questions, then make up a 'what if' list of possibles.

The interview itself
Checklist

- Forget that thousands of people are listening in. Be conversational. Remember you are talking to individuals.
- Paint pictures for them. As in presentations, use your voice to keep interest and attention.
- Put a smile in your voice, sound enthusiastic about what you are saying.
- Ignore the microphone and speak in your normal voice.
- Think before you speak to avoid, 'ums' and 'ahs' also avoid clichés and jargon words.
- Remove any distractions, e.g. jewellery, pens.
- Use note cards to write points, e.g. statistics. Keep these to a minimum.
- Anticipate questions.
- Relax and do some deep breathing exercises before you begin.
- For both radio and television – check that the interviewer has your details correct e.g. your name, your company name.

Television
Remember 'First Impressions Last'.

Television is the most powerful weapon of mass communication we have. Unlike radio, we have to consider very carefully how we appear to others. Our clothes must be appropriate for the occasion, and our body language must be positive. On arrival at the studio, make-up is necessary to allow for the intense lighting and for the heat it generates.

It is useful to know which camera is transmitting at any given moment – this is indicated by a red light. Ignore the camera, and give eye contact to the interviewer. Television favours a relaxed, intimate style, therefore our body language should match this.

- Practise a comfortable seating position – hands relaxed in lap.
- Keep your head still and smile appropriately.
- Control your hands – no patting hair, rubbing nose etc.

- Give eye contact to the interviewer.
- Keep a calm countenance – remember that the camera may be on you when you grimace. Smile when appropriate and aim to look pleasant.
- Keep your head up (otherwise in poor lighting, you will appear to have shadows under your eyes).
- Keep positive and enthusiastic – put your points across clearly and concisely.

Telephone Interview

Questions to ask the journalist:

- Why is the article being written?
- What is the angle?
- Why have you been approached?
- Who else is being interviewed?

Many of the same rules apply as to any other interview.

- Give the journalist only the information which you want to be used.
- Keep to key points.
- Spell out any unusual names.
- Check that they have your personal details accurately (your name, your company name, etc.)

If you are being interviewed face-to-face, have a written summary of your key points/details to leave with the interviewer.

What to Wear on Television – Basic Do's and Don'ts

- Select something from your wardrobe that reflects your professional image and with which you are comfortable.
- Don't wear clothes with lumpy textures, such as bulky tweeds, or novelty weaves that might expand or exaggerate on camera.

- Rely on familiar fashion classics rather than extreme high fashion or trendy garments that might divert attention.
- Avoid clothes such as recreational sportswear or evening wear, when they do not complement your normal occupational role.
- Choose clothes with subdued colours that do not overpower your natural skin tone.
- Avoid colours that blend into those of the studio set and lighting conditions. If possible, bring along an alternative outfit to avoid this.
- Avoid curiosities in jewellery or accessories that might divert attention from your message.
- Choose small accessories (earrings for women, cuff-links for men) which enhance your clothes.
- Don't wear accessories that are large, move too much, glare, or make a noise.
- Keep your hairstyle simple, making sure it does not obscure your face from different camera angles.
- Don't use exaggerated make-up. Be guided by the station make-up artist or on-camera station personnel.
- When possible, call the station in advance for guidance on the colour and tonality of your on-air clothing.

Social Occasion

After-Dinner Speeches

These can last between ten minutes and forty-five minutes. One of the advantages of this sort of presentation is that your audience are generally supportive and in good spirits. The number of speeches after a dinner can vary, so do your preparation (which should now be second nature to you): find out everything you need to know. If there are several speakers it is probably in your interest to speak early on when the audience are more receptive. A short speech tends to work best. Keep it simple, with just a few key points.

After-dinner speeches are supposed to be entertaining, so keep it lighthearted. This is one occasion where a relevant joke or two may go down well, provided you are confident that they will be well received.

Avoid risqué jokes on these occasions, particularly the sexist or racist variety, which usually turn out to be embarrassing for everyone!

Particular areas to add to your preparation list:

- It is important for after-dinner speakers to check what style of dress is appropriate.
- At dinner, eat slowly and lightly in order to avoid indigestion or that bloated feeling. Avoid alcohol completely until after your speech.
- Relate to your audience: whether speaking to the cricket club, Chamber of Commerce, Rotary, Burns Supper, tell some amusing anecdotes, using original material.
- Keep material brief and entertaining – leave them wanting more!
- See section on notes (after dinner).
- This is an enjoyable occasion – be prepared – relax and enjoy yourself.

14. Questions and Answers

Here are the ten most frequently asked questions on my training course:

Q. Should I include humour in my presentation?

A. When used correctly, humour is worth including in most types of presentation. It can lighten a heavy subject, relax the audience, and keep them alert. However, the presenter always takes a risk when using humour. If it is not successful everyone feels foolish. Try to use humour that will produce inward chuckles and smiles from your audience, rather than side-splitting laughs – an appropriate light-hearted quotation rather than a long joke. Appropriate humour adds the occasional light touch, and will help freshen your presentation material – perhaps making your audience more receptive to the important messages.
See Introductions and Conclusions, Chapter 4)

Q. In the future I will be involved in formal presentations. Is there a correct form of address?

A. Many meetings nowadays are less formal than in the past, however many still begin with a formal address, which helps you, the presenter and also the audience. It is an easy to remember format for you to get started – which is always the worst part in public speaking. It also gives the audience time to 'tune in' to your voice.

- In many cases, a straightforward 'Mr (or Madam) Chairman, Ladies and Gentlemen' will suffice.
- If you are dealing with special guests, and titled guests, it is best to check with the organisers.
- Always start a formal address by addressing the chair; the only exception to this is when royalty is present. The following are suitable: 'Mr (or Madam) Chairman'; 'Mr President'

Then any special guests can be mentioned. Normally if there are any peers present who have not been named as special guests – follow with 'My Lords (and Ladies)' . . .

The remainder of the audience is address by 'Ladies and Gentlemen' or Ladies', 'Gentlemen', if a single sex audience.

Other exceptions may be the address to members of specific groups, for example, 'Fellow Members', 'Fellow Scots' – whatever is appropriate. (see Introduction, Chapter 3)

Q. Is is better to prepare more material than one needs?

A. I believe it's a good idea when presenting to:

1) Large groups: There tend to be less interruptions in large groups, and material can often run out before your time is up. Prepare extra material to fill any possible time gap.
2) Small groups: More audience interruption, therefore time is usually used up more quickly. Prepare and reserve extra material for question time. See Putting it together, Chapter 6)

Q. Do you think it's a good idea to keep notes, and other presentation source material for future use?

A. It is a very good idea. To start a presentation fact file, use one of the storage boxes mentioned in the visual aids chapter. Alternatively, you could use the expanding type of file folder with pockets arranged in alphabetical order, or an index card box. Collect clippings of things that amuse you from magazines and newspapers. Also source material, surveys, shocking statistics, amazing facts, ideas for visuals.

After you attend a presentation as a guest:

- Write a brief synopsis. For example, type of audience, questions asked, type of approach, visuals, anecdotes which were received well by the audience.

Do the same thing after you give a presentation. Remember to jot down questions which you couldn't answer, or material which you should have included in your presentation and didn't.

Keeping this simple record will help you build up a useful resource for future reference. If you also file your 'invitations to speak' (and any other feedback on your performance) this material can provide you with testimonials. It will help you to avoid duplicating material should you receive a repeat invitation to speak to a particular group.

(See Preparation, Chapter 3)

Q. What should I do about people who sit and chat through my presentation?

A. Remember the key role when dealing with your audience – **be polite**. To continue speaking while others talk shows inexperience and also invites attention.

You could:

- Pause – and look directly at the offenders. This will usually silence them.
- Pause, smile and say to them: 'I'm sorry to disturb you . . .' This usually gets a chuckle. The audience appreciates you intervening, as persistent talkers are annoying for everyone.

(See Questions, Chapter 11)

Q. I like to see the time when presenting. Should I take off my watch, or keep it on?

A. This is purely a matter of choice. Many meeting rooms have wall mounted clocks facing the presenter. This is useful as the audience will not be aware that you are clock watching. Some presenters take off their watch, or use a small travel clock placed on the table in front of them. This works well, provided that it is placed discreetly and not seen by the audience. Don't draw attention to it, unlike one presenter who picked up his watch, put it to his ear and gave it a good shake. Take a leaf out of Queen Elizabeth's book. She wears her watch on her right wrist facing inwards. When she holds out her arm, to shake hands, she knows exactly what time it is!

(See Timing, Chapter 6)

Q. Are there any rules about dress?

A. If you are not certain what kind of dress is appropriate for the function ask the organisers well in advance. If this is not possible, if in doubt, it is better to be over-dressed than under-dressed. Also, err towards the conventional.

(See the section on dress in Chapter 9)

Q. Is it OK to have a hand in my pocket when presenting?

A. Of all the body parts, hands seem to give presenters the most problems. There are no hard and fast rules to this question of hands in pockets. I have seen good and bad examples. However, I would advise keeping hands out of pockets altogether, for the following reasons:

- It looks slovenly and not professional
- You will probably need your hands, to hold cards, gesture, etc.
- You may play with loose change, keys in your pocket.

Lastly, you simply look more confident and competent when your audience can see your hands.

(See Body Language, Chapter 9.)

Q. How should I address individuals in the group, first names, full names, etc.?

A. Completing your audience profile can help with this problem. Then, depending on the formality or informality of the occasion, you could use either address.

In a small group, the intimate atmosphere means that you can use first names if appropriate: 'As you know, Jim, your marketing director, has asked me along today to . . .' Remember to check the company style. There are still many companies where first names are not used, even between managers and staff.

In the small group situation participants are often asked to write their names on place cards or name badges. If you intend being informal and using first names, for example, guide your audience: 'This is an informal session today, so could you please write your first name only on the card in front of you.' Also supply suitable marker pens, otherwise you will get illegible names in pencil or biro.

Q. What do you consider the most important element for successful presentation?

A. Without a doubt, I would recommend preparation. 'To fail to prepare is to prepare to fail'.

The three 'P's' fulfil all requirements:

1. Preparation
2. PMA (Positive mental attitude)
3. Practice

Thorough preparation, an enthusiastic approach to your subject, followed by lots of practice, will provide you with the basis to make every performance a successful presentation.

15. Advice from the experts

This final section contains advice from 20 men and women in the world of business, the media, politics and entertainment, who all excel in successful presentation.

I have chosen a variety of views which complement the advice in this book. These are the qualities they believe are worth developing:

Dr Marjorie Mowlam, MP
Appearance: Personal appearance – sadly, people judge what you say by how you look.

Mrs Yve Newbold, Company Secretary, Hanson plc
Autocue: There is a very good method used by the front bench in the House of Commons whereby the whole script is prepared in advance. The speaker needs a lot of practice, ideally with video, to be able to read the script whilst looking up at the audience for quite long periods. The full script of what one is going to say reduces nerves to manageable proportions.

Godfrey Smith, *Sunday Times* columnist
Clarity: Easy to say, terribly hard to pull off (with it goes that other cardinal rule – brevity)

Sir John Harvey-Jones, MBE, Chairman Parallax Ent., writer, broadcaster
Confidence: Even though the presenter may not feel it. Humour and originality.

Peter Jay, writer, broadcaster, Economic and Business editor, BBC
Communication: Ability to communicate: This simply means fluency and vocabulary. There are no important TV techniques; just be your own bright, intelligent and communicative self.

Ludovic Kennedy, writer, broadcaster, presenter
Control: Good presenters have pleasing voices, are in control of their material and display a natural authority.

Clare Francis, author
Feedback – Be ruthlessly self-critical. Make tapes of your voice – eradicate irritating habits. Examine video tapes of your performance and be prepared to learn from them.

Sir Peter Ustinov, actor, dramatist, film director
Feeling: It is essential to give the impression your words are felt rather than learnt; not as easy as it seems. Most politicians stumble at this hurdle, for the simple reason that their texts were written by someone else.

Emma Nicholson, MP
Friendly: A smiling face – cheerfulness is catching; they'll want to take you on in preference to someone gloomy.

Anne Hooper, writer, radio broadcaster
Honesty: Admit mistakes when you make them and make no bones about repeating something correctly. This sounds better than flustered confusion.

Margaret Ewing MP
Impact: Know in advance what your opening and closing remarks will be. Opening remarks are very important – all of us get nervous about starting, so confidence is critical. Closing remarks are important because they leave a final impression; what is said in between is often lost.

Jane Asher, writer, actress
Nerves: Everyone gets nervous – it would be unnatural if you didn't, but remember that your audience wants to hear you. They're not against you.

Rosie Barnes, ex-MP
Notes: Know your subject well enough to be able to speak without notes. Use only headlines. However, have notes to hand as a safety net, in case you dry up.

Sir Robin Day, TV broadcaster, interviewer
Personality: Including e.g. authority, presence, charm, wit and guts.

Valerie Grove, writer, interviewer, *Sunday Times*
Professionalism: Intelligence, mastery of the subject, warmth and enthusiasm.

Joanna Lumley, actress
Rapport: Be friendly, be determined to enjoy yourself. People are only people.

Janet Suzman, actress
Sincerity: Know your subject and be yourself.

Rosabeth Moss Kanter, Professor, Harvard University
Style: People are more interested in substance than style, and style is something that can be cultivated later. But if you have nothing to say, that certainly shows. For any group that is not yet well accepted in the workplace and has to prove that people who are members of that particular group belong and have credibility, there is no substitute for the certainty of clear knowledge.

Edwina Currie, MP
Voice: You need to learn how to use the microphone, or if there is no mike, how to ensure everyone present can hear. It helps if they can see you – so stand up. Don't mumble and keep your head up.

16. Conclusion

As stated in the foreword, this book is for everyone who has to present. The ideas included have been tried and tested by the many business people who have decided to improve their communication skills.

Much can be learned from reading a 'how to' book and successful presentation is no exception. However, having learned the skills there is no substitute for putting them into practice.

If you would like further advice on training, either individual or in-house, please contact:

Communication Works Ltd.
47 Marloes Road
LONDON W8 6LA
Tel: 071 938 2025

Meanwhile I wish you enjoyable and successful presentations.

Index

action needs, 6
active listening, 149-52, 182
   barriers to, 151-2
after-dinner speaking, 72, 198-9
agenda, format, 187-8
agreements, use of, 53, 59
alcohol, 51
anecdotes, use of, 22-3, 36
appearance (see also dress), 129-30
Asher, Jane, 87-8, 207
audience, 3-5, 10-15
   belief-changing, 5
   belief-strengthening, 5
   body language, 129
   effective communication with, 48-62
   emphasising relevance to, 23
   forms of address, 204
   foreign, 178-80
   impact, creation of, 32-47
   information about, 11-12
   information needs of, 4-5
   problem behaviour, 160-63, 202
   questions from (see also question and answer sessions), 145-63
   retention of information (table), 42
   types of, 157-8
audience participation, 37
audience profile, 12-15
audience types, dealing with, 157-63
Autocue (teleprompter), 80-82

Barnes, Rosie, 207
behaviourial styles, 164-70
belief-changing, 5
belief-strengthening, 5
Blake, William, 101
Bob Says Opportunity Knocks, 90
body language, 96, 112-130, 203
   distance from audience, 121-2
   expression, 118-20
   eye contact, 117-18
   facial expression, 117
   gesture, 116-17
   hands, 120-21
   humorous application, 114
   image projection, 125
   positive attitude, 122-4
   posture, 114-16
'brainstorming', 16-18, 185-6

chairmanship, 180-92
Churchill, Winston, 22, 171
Cleese, John, 140
communication, effective, 48-62
communication test, 97-8
Communication Works (company), 25
company brochures, 55, 61
comparisons and contrasts, use of, 36
competitive presentations, 175-8
conclusions, 20, 39-41
   convincing, 40
   informative, 40
   summary of (approach to), 46-7
contracts, use of, 53, 59
Coward, Noel, 126
Currie, Edwina (MP), 207

Daily Mail, 85
Daily Mirror, 85
Daily Telegraph, 85
Day, Sir Robin, 207
demonstrations, 37, 38
directives, 53, 58
discussions (see also meetings), 190-92
   guiding skills, 192
   problem-solving, 170
   starting skills, 191
   stopping skills, 192
dress, 126-30, 203
   dressing for television interviews, 197-8

Einstein, Dr. Albert, 149
environment (see also venue), 49-50
Ewing, Margaret (MP), 206
examples,
   clarification of, 40
   use of, 27, 36, 38
eye contact (see also body language), 117-18

foreign audience, 178-80
formal meetings,
    form of address at, 200-201
forms, 59-60
Francis, Clare, 206

Glass, Dr Lillian, 94
Grove, Valerie, 207
Guardian, 85
guiding skills, 192

Hansard, 188
Harvard Business School, 3
Harvey-Jones, Sir John (MBE), 22, 205
'hooks', 21-2, 24
Hooper, Anne, 206
humour, use of, 22-3, 25-7, 200

image projection (*see also* body language), 125
impact, 32-47
    methods, 44-5
information,
    about audience, 11-12
    editing of, 18
    gathering, 16-20
    presentation of, 11
in-house communications, 54-5, 60
interference, 49-50
interviews (*see* media interviews)
introductions, 20-25, 37-9
    informative, 38-9
    summary of, 45-6

Jay, Peter, 206

Kennedy, John F., 107
Kennedy, Ludovic, 206

Lamb, Charles, 23
language (*see also* speech), 50-51
leading a meeting, 180-94
leading group discussions (*see also* meetings), 190-92
lecturing, 172-3
letters and memoranda, use of, 51-2, 56
lighting (*see also* venue), 28
Lumley, Joanna, 207

Macmillan, Harold, 116
Maltz, Maxwell, 123
manuals, 54, 59

media interviews, 194-8
    preparation for, 195
    telephone interviews, 197
    television interviews, 196, 197, 198
meetings,
    chairmanship, 180-92
    formal, form of address at, 200-201
    leading, 180-94
    minute-taking, 188-9
    planning for, 189-90
    roles adopted in, 193-4
    staff meetings, 188
Mehabrian, Albert, 93
memos,
    as alternative to presentation, 4
microphone, use of, 107-11
    advantages, 108
    disadvantages, 109
    technique, 107
Monkhouse, Bob, 90
Morgan, Peter (Director General, Institute of Directors), 18
Morris, Stewart, 90
Moss Kanter, Rosabeth (Harvard Business School), 3, 4, 108, 207
Mowlam, Dr Marjorie (MP), 205

nervousness, 86-92
    causes of, 86-7
    effects of, 86
    overcoming, 86-92
    relaxation methods, 88-9
    shaking, 90
    visualisation techniques, 87-8
Newbold, Mrs Y.M. (Company Secretary, Hanson plc), 118, 205
Nicholson, Emma (MP), 206
notes, 63-85
    Autocue (teleprompter), use of, 80-82
    cards as prompts, 71
        for after-dinner speaking, 72
    editing ideas, 63-6
    preparation of, 72-3
    script, use of, 74-85
        cues for visual aids, 77
    structuring, 67-71
    text layout, 75-7

objectives,
    agreed, 9
    measurable, 9
    realistic, 10

Index

timely, 10

Pascale, Blaise, 128
Pirates of Penzance, The, 105
posture (*see also* body language), 114–16
preparation, 16–31
   additional material, 201
   checklist, 27–8
   notes (*see separate entry*)
   unexpected, the, 30–1
presentation,
   alternative types of, 171–99
   body of, 20
   clients, for, 175–8
   competitive presentations, 175–8
   conclusions (*see separate entry*)
   engaging audience, 3
   establishing objectives, 8–10
   formulating ideas, 35–7
   'hooks', 21–2, 24
   humour, use of, 22–3, 36, 200
   impact of, 32–47
   interference, 49–50
   introductions (*see separate entry*)
   key elements of, 7–15
   length of, 18
   need for, 6
   nervousness (*see separate entry*)
   notes (*see separate entry*)
   reading style, 80
   repetition, use of, 43
   reprise and close of (*see* conclusions)
   script, use of, 74–85
   seating layout, 29, 49
   speech (*see separate entry and* speaking)
   structure of (*see* structure)
   style of, 164–70
   technical presentations, 174–5
   timing of, 73–4
   value of, 6
   venue, 28, 29, 49–50
   visual aids (*see separate entry*)
presenter
   alcohol, 51
   answering questions (*see also* question and answer sessions), 155–6
   body language (*see separate entry*)
   dress (*see separate entry*)
   qualities of, 1–6
   question and answer sessions (*see separate entry*)
   style of, 164–70

voice (*see* speaking, speech)
presenting a paper, 174
Presenting for Women (by Carole McKenzie), 4
problem behaviour, 160–63, 202
   aggression, 161
   attacking, 163
   blocking, 160
   confession, 161
   distracting, 161
   dominating, 160
   'know-it-alls', 162
   manipulating, 161
   monopolising, 162
   nitpicking, 162
   rationalising, 162
   seeking status, 161
   show-offs, 162
   special pleading, 161
   timid, 162
   withdrawing, 161
problem solving, 170
professional papers, 55–6, 61–2
proposals, use of, 52, 57

question and answer sessions, 145–63
   after presentation, 146–7
      advantages/disadvantages, 147
   answering questions, 155–6
   during presentation, 146–7
      advantages/disadvantages, 147
   preparation for, 145–6, 148–9
   when to allow, 146–7
questions
   after presentation, 146–7
   as introduction, 23
   closed, 154
   direct, 23
   during presentation, 146–7
   follow-up, 154
   handling, 159
   open-ended, 154
   rhetorical, 23, 43
   types of, for presenter, 154
quotations, use of, 22, 38
   in conclusion, 40

rate of speech test, 82–3
readability test, 83–5
reading style, aids to, 80
receivers (*see* audience)

relaxation methods (*see also* nervousness), 88–9
reports, use of, 52, 56–7
Richardson, Sir Ralph, 92
room layout (*see also* venue), 29

script, use of (*see also* notes), 74–85
seating plan, 29, 49
sincerity, 2–3
Smith, Godfrey, 205
speaking,
    extemporaneous, 171–2
    impromptu, 171
speech, 50–51, 93–111
    communication test, 97–8
    diction, 98–9, 104–5
    exercises for the tongue, 102–3
    intonation, 79–80
    microphone, 107–11
        advantages, 108
        disadvantages, 109
        technique, 107
    modulation, 99
    nasal, 103
    pitch, 103
    projection, 99–102
    rate of delivery, 104
    relaxation exercises, 105
    slurring, 102
    survey of talking habits, 94
    vocal technique, 106
staff meetings, 188
statistics, use of, 27, 36, 38
stories, use of, 22–3, 36
structure, 18–21, 32–47
    flexibility in, 26–7
    logical approaches to, 32–4
        key elements structure, 33
        problem-analysis-solution structure, 34
        proposition-proof-conclusion, 34
        space structure, 33
        time structure, 33
    psychological approaches to, 32, 34–5
        brief to action, 35
        common to uncommon, 35
Sun, The, 85
Sunday Times Business News, 85
Suzman, Janet, 207

technical presentations, 174–5
telephone interviews (*see also* media interviews), 197
teleprompter (Autocue), 80–82
television interviews (*see also* media interviews), 196–8
    dressing for, 197–8
timing, 73–4
Twain, Mark, 87

Ustinov, Sir Peter, 130, 206

ventilation (*see also* venue), 28
venue, 28, 29, 49–50
Video Arts (training films), 140
visual aids, 38, 40, 42, 77, 131–44
    bar graphs, 140
    chalkboards/blackboards, 137
        advantages/disadvantages, 144
    charts, 139
    cueing, 77
    display boards, 137–8
    flannel boards, 137
    flipcharts, 134–5
        advantages/disadvantages, 144
    flowcharts, 139
    handouts, 138–9
    line graphs, 140
    magnetic boards, 137
    models, 136
    organisational charts, 140
    overhead projection (OHPS), 131
        advantages/disadvantages, 143
        storage of transparencies, 142
    pie charts, 139–40
    pointer, use of, 141
    props, 138
        advantages/disadvantages, 144
    slides (35mm), 132–4
        advantages/disadvantages, 144
    video/film, 132
    whiteboards, 136
        advantages/disadvantages, 144
visualisation techniques (*see also* nervousness), 87–8
vocal technique (*see also* speech, speaking), 106

Whitehorn, Katherine, 87

'signposting', 24–5
'smart' objectives, 8–10